ADVANCE PRAISE FOR *SCENES AND SEQUELS*

"Indispensable nuts-and-bolts advice for crafting successful fiction. Highly recommended." — Evan Marshall, co-creator of *The Marshall Plan® Novel Writing Software*

"I am a huge fan of Jack Bickham's classic craft book *Scene & Structure*, and consider it one of three essential books to a writer's library. When I learned of Mike Klaassen's new book, *Scenes & Sequels*, and its efforts to expand upon Bickham's work, I looked forward to reading it with great anticipation. Well, it doesn't disappoint! It's a great addition to Bickham's initial explanation of the two most important elements of story and delivers both an in-depth explanation of these elements and an important expansion of the principles it delivered. Highly recommended for serious writers." — Les Edgerton, Author of *Finding Your Voice* and *Hooked*.

ALSO BY MIKE KLAASSEN

YOUNG-ADULT NOVELS

The Brute

Cracks

HISTORICAL FICTION

Backlash: A War of 1812 Novel

NONFICTION

Fiction-Writing Modes: Eleven essential tools for bringing your story to life

SCENES AND SEQUELS
How to Write Page-Turning Fiction

by Mike Klaassen

Pennsauken, New Jersey

Scenes and Sequels: How to write page-turning fiction

Cover design by Toelke Associates

© 2016 Michael John Klaassen

Published by Bookbaby, Pennsauken, NJ

ISBN: 978-1-68222-907-1 (Print)
ISBN: 978-1-68222-908-8 (eBook)

Dedicated to two champions of the concept of writing fiction with scenes and sequels: Dwight V. Swain (1915-1992) and Jack M. Bickham (1930-1997).

ACKNOWLEDGEMENTS

My first exposure to scenes and sequels was through *Scene & Structure: How to construct fiction with scene-by-scene flow, logic, and readability* (Writer's Digest Books) by Jack M. Bickham and *Techniques of a Selling Writer* (University of Oklahoma Press) by Dwight V. Swain.

I also wish to acknowledge the contribution of my wife of thirty-five years, Carol S. Klaassen (1951-2012), who not only inspired and encouraged me in writing this book but was also the first reader of early drafts of the manuscript.

TABLE OF CONTENTS

PREFACE

What do the following novels have in common?

- *Hatchet* by Gary Paulsen
- *One for the Money* by Janet Evanovich
- *Ender's Game* by Orson Scott Card
- *American Assassin* by Vince Flynn
- *Twilight* by Stephenie Meyer
- *The General's Daughter* by Nelson DeMille
- *The Client* by John Grisham
- *A Cry in the Night* by Mary Higgins Clark
- *The Lucky One* by Nicholas Sparks
- *The Da Vinci Code* by Dan Brown

These novels share many attributes: memorable characters, engaging plot, interesting setting, resonating theme, and appropriate style. Each is a "page turner" that grips you from the opening lines and commands your attention until the end.

A closer look also reveals that these books include both scenes and sequels. Full disclosure: I have never communicated with any of the authors listed above; I have no way of knowing whether they support the concept of writing with scenes and sequels or if they intentionally use them when they write. I just know that my analysis reveals that both scenes and sequels are an important part of the structure of the novels listed above. To me that raises the question of whether the rest of us are making optimal use of scenes and sequels in our own writing.

The value of scenes in fiction is widely accepted, and for good reason. Scenes propel the story forward, and they include the exciting, sexy, explosive parts of a story. You may be less familiar with the concept of sequels, so let's take a closer look.

Imagine you have written two great scenes that nicely move your story forward. In the first scene the focal character attempts to accomplish a short-term goal that he hopes will bring him closer to achieving his primary objective in the story. He encounters resistance that knocks him so far back that he is even farther from achieving his goal than when he started the scene. The second scene shows the character pursuing an entirely different course of action. This raises numerous questions:

- How did the character react emotionally to the devastating setback of the previous scene—or is he an emotionless, cardboard character?
- What was the character's thought process for determining his new course of action—or did he make a thoughtless snap decision?
- Did the character consider alternative courses of action—or did he impulsively go with the first solution that came to mind?
- Among several potential courses of action, did the character weigh the alternatives—or did he conveniently pick the one that the author needed to write the next scene?

You may be writing great scenes, but if they are not coupled where appropriate with sequels, you may be missing up to half of your storytelling firepower. If you are not intimately familiar with sequels, you may also lack sufficient understanding of scenes and how to unlock their full potential. This book provides you with the know-how needed to fully develop both scenes and sequels.

Who should read this book? If you are a beginning novelist, this book will help you build a foundation of practical knowledge that might otherwise take many years of self-study or trial and error to accumulate. If you are an experienced writer, the information in this book may provide you with information that helps you take your writing to new heights or sustains it in the face of ever-increasing competition.

Fiction writers tend to fall into one of three camps: (1) *outliners*, who plan their work in detail prior to writing, (2) *free spirits*, who like to jump in and see where inspiration and instinct lead, and (3) *tweeners*, those somewhere in between. Each of these styles has merit, and all three have drawbacks. Regardless of which style you use to create your first draft, you still face the challenge of polishing your manuscript into a seamless story. That's where a thorough understanding of scenes and sequels can really pay off: turning a mess into a work of art.

I'm the author of two young-adult novels, a historical novel set during the War of 1812, and a nonfiction book about the craft of writing fiction. I've been a student of the craft of writing fiction for many years, have read dozens of books on the subject, and have written many articles about writing fiction. My experience as a novelist and my study of the craft of writing fiction have given me a great appreciation for the value of writing both scenes and sequels.

If you're like me, sometimes you feel overwhelmed by the challenge of writing the kind of fiction that stands out in today's highly competitive market. I have over a hundred books about the craft of writing fiction in my library, and I've studied each one thoroughly. What I found was a huge amount of information, but much of it is incomplete, disorganized, and inconsistent. As I gained a better understanding of how the parts fit together, I found that writing about fiction helped clarify my thinking. I'm pleased to share what I have learned.

Of the many books I've studied, only two paid much attention to scenes and sequels: *Techniques of a Selling Writer* (1965) by Dwight V. Swain (1915-1992) and *Scene and Structure* (1993) by Jack M. Bickham (1930-1997). I encourage you to read both. Swain and Bickham provide a solid base from which to build an understanding of scenes and sequels, but much has been learned about fiction since each wrote his book. I used Swain and Bickham as a starting point, gathered concepts and terminology from others, and added to that body of work from my own research and observation.

My goal in writing this book is to present to you the most comprehensive and concise analysis of scenes and sequels available anywhere. That information puts you a giant step closer to bringing your writing to its full potential.

This book is like no other book about writing fiction. No matter how familiar you are with the concept of scenes, this book will provide you with a greater understanding of writing them. You will gain a deep understanding and appreciation for sequels and their potential. You will learn how to troubleshoot your manuscript, blasting through writer's block in the process. Lastly, you will see how to put all the pieces together to write page-turning fiction.

NOTE TO READERS: NAMES AND DEFINITIONS MATTER

You may be calling scenes and sequels by different names. What are the correct names for what I refer to as scenes and sequels? And does it really matter? As writers we take pride in finding the right word for each situation, so it's pretty hard to argue that the labels we use are not important. But that isn't the most important reason to correctly label scenes and sequels. Failure to adequately name something can reflect a lack of understanding (whales, at one time, were classified as fish). Understanding something isn't just an academic exercise. Understanding a writing technique improves our ability to use that tool to its full potential, in writing and in teaching.

Let's explore scenes first. The term *scene* is one of many in the English language that takes on different meaning in different contexts. A *scene* can represent a place where an event occurred, as in *scene of the crime*. A *scene* can represent an exhibition of passionate or explosive emotion, as in *making a scene*. In dramatic presentations (such as in theater, movies, and television), *scene* can mean the stage itself or the surroundings amid which drama is presented; or a *scene* can mean a sequence of events within the presentation.[1]

How-to books about writing fiction range widely in their coverage of the subject of scenes. Some don't use the term *scene* at all. Others promote the concept of writing scenes without attempting to define *scene*, or they define the term with vague, rambling expressions.

When I started studying the craft of writing fiction, I was first exposed to the concept of scenes by Jack M. Bickham (1930-1997) in *Scene and Structure* (1993). Bickham gives much credit to his teacher and friend Dwight V. Swain (1915-1992), who wrote *Techniques of a Selling Writer* (1965).

Often we can learn more about a subject if we can properly define it. Swain defined a scene as "a unit of conflict lived through by character and reader."[2] Bickham apparently recognized a need to expand on Swain's definition because he described a *scene* as "a segment of story action, written moment-by-moment, without summary, presented onstage in the story 'now.'"[3]

Each of these definitions has merit, but they lack the clarity and conciseness needed to be useful tools. Let's get basic, here. What are we referring to? Swain refers to a scene as a "unit," but he doesn't say unit of what. Bickham describes scenes as a "segment of story action."

Swain and Bickham were pioneers in the study of scenes and sequels. We owe them much, but that doesn't mean their work can't be improved. Both were teachers, and I suspect they would be pleased to have their concepts refined and expanded.

To fully understand scenes, we need to look at the bigger picture of where they fit as structural units in written fiction. Words form phrases and sentences. Sentences comprise paragraphs. Two or more paragraphs with some common purpose are referred to as *passages* or *segments* of writing. Scenes could easily include two or more paragraphs, so it's fair to define them as either passages or segments. Let's start our definition of scenes with the phrase "A passage of writing that . . ."

Now let's address the "that" in the above definition. What's the *that* in a scene? The Swain and Bickham definitions of a scene include references to conflict, character, reader, story, action, moment-by-moment, on stage, and the "story now." *Scenes* are sometimes referred to as units of drama, so I would add tension and suspense to the list. Rather than a concise definition, these terms seem to be more of a description of what an ideal scene *should* include.

To be helpful in troubleshooting our own writing, we need a definition that boils a scene down to its essence. Swain's "unit of conflict" seems to come pretty close, but *conflict* is a compound concept that includes a character attempting to achieve a goal and encountering resistance that puts accomplishment of that goal in doubt. Resistance without a character and a goal would be meaningless. The pure essence of a scene focuses on its lowest common denominator: a character attempting to achieve a goal. With that in mind, I define a *scene* as a passage of writing in which a character attempts to achieve a goal.

Now let's look at sequels. The Latin origin of the word *sequel* means *to follow*. *Sequel* can refer to people who follow, such as retainers. A *sequel* can mean next in an unfolding series, such as *Jaws III*. *Sequel* can also mean something that follows from an antecedent cause.[4]

Other than the two by Swain and Bickham, few how-to books mention sequels. If they refer to the concept at all, they use terms like contemplative scenes, transition scenes, reaction scenes, reaction sections, scene setups, reflective passages, or aftermaths.

Swain defined a *sequel* as "a unit of transition that links two scenes."[5] Bickham described *transition* as "a very simple device which provides a direct statement to the reader to the effect that a change in time, place or viewpoint has happened since the last scene."[6]

Bickham continues, "Such simple transitions sometimes are enough to serve as the bridge to carry your reader from one scene to another. But clearly, if you want to deal in any depth with a character's emotional state, or show his thought processes as he analyzes his plight and makes future plans, or use his thinking process to give the reader information about things that happened before the story started (or in the time that lapsed between chapters), then you need something bigger and better than a simple transition. . . That "something"—the sequel—is the glue that holds scenes together and helps you get from one to the next."[7]

I cringe at Bickham's reference to transitions as "a very simple device." My book *Fiction-Writing Modes* identifies transitions as one of the eleven modes and devotes a full chapter to the subject. Admittedly, many writers of how-to books downplay the importance of transitions. Bickham does do us a big favor by noting the relationship between the subjects of discussion: *scene—transition—sequel*. In this book, we'll leave the discussion of transitions at that.

Let's define a sequel. If a scene is a passage of writing, so is a sequel, so let's start our definition of *sequel* as "a passage of writing . . ." But what is the *that* in a sequel? Bickham describes a sequel as having three phases: emotion, thinking, and decision. That encompasses a lot, so let's boil it down even more. Clearly, a *sequel* is a reaction to the ending of a scene, so my definition includes the phrase ". . . in which the character reacts to the resolution of a scene." But this definition would seem to include a physical reaction, and if a passage is about a character's physical reaction, then it is probably a scene rather than a sequel. While a sequel may include incidental activity, a sequel is mostly in the character's mind, so I've added the word *reflects* to the definition. I define a *sequel* as a passage of fiction in which a character reflects on the resolution of a scene.

Swain and Bickham both used the terms *scene* and *sequel*, and they wrote comprehensively on these subjects, more so than anyone else I've read. Sometimes in recent years, the terms *scene* and *sequel* have been at least partially replaced with the terms *proactive scene* and *reflective scene*. As writers we value the preciseness of words, so why is it better to replace the single term *scene* with the phrase *proactive scene*, using two words? Why is it better to replace the single term *sequel* with the phrase *reactive scene*?—especially without defining *scene* first.

I believe the use of the terms *proactive scene* and *reactive scene* reflects a fundamental misunderstanding of the concept of scenes in the structure of fiction writing. The use of *proactive* and *reactive* as modifiers implies that they are subsets of a larger category called *scene*. If so, how is that term defined? How would the term incorporate passages that include elements of both proactive and reactive scenes and passages that are neither proactive nor reactive scenes? Difficult isn't it? I suspect that's why the proponents of the terms *proactive* and *reactive* don't bother to define *scene*.

As I mentioned earlier, this discussion is not merely academic because our goal is to develop a useful technique for writing and teaching. A helpful tool for understanding fiction would be to have a comprehensive model of how fiction writing works. The definitions I have presented for scenes and sequels fit into a useful model of how fiction works.

CHAPTER 1: SCENES, PART I

CHAPTER CONTENTS

- Elements of fiction
- Plot structure
- Structural units of fiction writing
- Ebb and flow of fiction
- Components of a scene

Nothing generates page-turning fiction better than a well-told scene. This chapter delves into the concept of scenes, but before we get into specifics we need to make sure we are using the same terminology. For your convenience I've included a practical glossary of fiction-writing terms at the back of this book. Let's also examine a few concepts that put scenes and sequels in context.

ELEMENTS OF FICTION

This book is about a specific aspect of writing fiction, but having a panoramic view of fiction as a whole also will be helpful.

Five fundamental elements comprise all fiction: character, plot, setting, theme, and style. Each has its own function within a story:

1. *Plot* is the *what* (or *what happens*).

2. *Character* is the *who*.

3. *Setting* is the *where* and *when*.

4. *Theme* is the *why*.

5. *Style* is the *how*.

PLOT STRUCTURE

Scene and sequel fit under the element of plot, which has structure at three distinct levels. On a microlevel, plot consists of stimulus and response (sometimes referred to as action and reaction). On a macrolevel, plot has a beginning, a middle, and an ending. But plot also has a midlevel structure: scene and sequel.

In the context of plot, a *scene* is a passage of writing in which a character attempts to achieve a goal. If a character is attempting to achieve an objective, then a scene logically ends with either success, failure, or some variation of either. A *sequel* is what happens next, the character's reflective response to a scene's resolution.

STRUCTURAL UNITS OF FICTION WRITING

We need to establish a common language regarding the *structural units of fiction writing*, the format for constructing fiction from individual words to a complete novel. No doubt you are familiar with much of the terminology, but the relationship between the units is also important.

The smallest units of writing are words, phrases, clauses, sentences, and paragraphs. Duh! But what do you call two or more paragraphs with some common purpose? For lack of a better term, we generally refer to such "chunks" of writing as *passages* or *segments* of writing.

A *chapter* is a segment of writing delineated by chapter breaks. We create chapter breaks by inserting a page break at the end of a chapter and by starting the next page with a chapter title partway down the page. The prologue and the epilogue are two specialized types of chapters.

A chapter may include one or more *sections*, passages separated by one or more section breaks. In manuscript format, a section break is marked with a blank line. In printed novels a section may be delineated with a blank line, a bar, or some other symbol, such as a squiggly line. Some novels, especially long ones, may be further divided into *books* or *parts*, each including two or more chapters.

Where do scenes and sequels fit as structural units of fiction writing? Remember the definitions of scenes and sequels? A *scene* is a passage of writing in which a character attempts to achieve a goal. A *sequel* is a passage of writing in which a character reflects on the resolution of a scene. Scenes and sequels are specialized passages of writing (i.e., subsets of the units we call passages of writing).

Each of these units has a role. As writers we need to recognize each one, know its purpose, and understand how to use it to construct our story. A chapter includes at least one passage of writing, but it may include many passages. Passages within a chapter may consist of (1) scenes, (2) sequels, (3) fragments of scenes and sequels, (4) passages that are neither scenes nor sequels, and (5) passages that include elements of both scenes and sequels.

EBB AND FLOW OF FICTION

Scenes and sequels work together. A scene propels the story forward. The sequel is a breather that allows the character to regroup, evaluate, and plan before moving on. If plot were an engine, scene and sequel would be the pistons thrusting forward and pulling back to turn the driveshaft.

The structure of a scene and a sequel are quite different, because they serve entirely different purposes. Many how-to books depict the rising action of a story as a jagged line, or stairway: the ascending lines represent scenes, while the descending lines represent sequels. A scene drives the story forward like a wave racing up the beach. A sequel pulls the wave back and gathers strength for the next scene to surge up the beach even farther than the previous scene. A novel without scenes would be boring, but without sequels, a story is just one event after another.

Now let's take an in-depth look at scenes.

SCENES

Scenes mimic real life. When we want to accomplish something worthwhile, we make a determined effort to achieve it. If we meet resistance, we try again and again until we either succeed or we fail.

Fiction-writing books mention at least a few of the following terms as being important to plot: tension, suspense, resolution, motivation, goals, stakes, obstacles, conflict, success, and failure. But none mentions *all* of these elements, nor do they explain how they work together as part of a scene. To more fully understand a scene, let's look at its components.

SETUP

A scene's setup establishes its setting, including time, especially in relation to the previous passage of writing. The setup shows the reader from whose viewpoint the scene is being told and that character's situation—the circumstances in which the scene starts.

The nature of the situation must narrow, if not eliminate, the character's ability to take an easy way out. A plot situation which limits a character's choices of action is referred to as its *crucible*.

A crucible may take many forms, including physical, mental, social, and temporal. A crucible may range in scope from tiny to immense. A crucible may encompass the entire story, or it may be specific to one or more scenes.

A physical crucible could be as small as an actual straight-jacket or as huge as the entire world. For example, the Cold War between the United States and the Soviet Union has been described as a gasoline-filled room in which archenemies faced off, each holding a box of matches. A character's sense of honor may create a line of behavior the character refuses to cross, regardless of the consequences. Victorian England is famous for its strict social norms, the violation of which was simply "not done," because the consequences could be one's "ruin." The "ticking clock" is an example of a temporal crucible in which the character faces a deadline or countdown that leaves him with a steadily dwindling amount of time to act.

Setups may be long or short, depending upon the needs of the story. When a scene follows a passage with the same setting, character, and situation, no setup may be needed.

CHARACTER

Scenes may have a variety of characters (major characters, minor characters, heroes, villains, viewpoint characters). In a scene we are most interested in the *focal character*, the person or entity who is attempting to accomplish a goal. The focal character may be the protagonist, a villain, a minor character—any character. For example, Dan Brown's *The Da Vinci Code* has two main characters, but the novel includes scenes focusing on a number of others.

Usually the focal character is also the *viewpoint character*, the person from whose perspective the scene is told. But sometimes the actions of a focal character are observed by (or narrated from the viewpoint of) a separate character. Examples include *Moby-Dick* (where Ishmael observes Captain Ahab), *Shane* (where eleven-year-old Bob Starett observes Shane), and *The Great Gatsby* (where Nick Carraway observes Jay Gatsby).

For the sake of simplicity throughout the remainder of this book, whenever I mention a scene's character, I'm referring to the focal character.

GOAL

Goals may be classified into two groups: long-term and short-term. The long-term goal in fiction is the character's ultimate objective for the story, the *story goal*. A story often has only one story goal (such as to solve a murder, to prevent an international disaster, or to fall in love).

For fiction to be interesting, the story goal must be significant, at least to the main character, and it must be large enough and complicated enough so that the character cannot quickly and easily achieve it. The story goal can be attained only by completing a number of smaller goals. In a children's story or a short story, the number of goals may be only one, while a novel may have dozens of short-term goals.

A *scene* is a passage of fiction in which a character attempts to achieve a short-term goal that he hopes will bring him closer to achieving the story goal. The short-term goal in a scene is the *scene goal*. Throughout the remainder of this book, a scene goal will be referred to simply as a goal or objective.

A character's goal may be stated or it may be implied. Here's an example of a stated goal (in italics):

> Lancelot removed his glove and slapped the dark knight, *challenging him to a joust.*

This example states Lancelot's goal (to challenge the dark knight). But mentioning the goal is not necessary if the reason for the character's action is apparent from the context of the passage. For example, if the passage is in the context of knights who sometimes challenge each other to jousts as a means of settling matters of honor, then stating the goal is unnecessary.

> Lancelot removed his glove and slapped the dark knight.

In the context described above, the goal is implied without being stated. When a character attempts to do something, you may assume his goal is to achieve that "something." The importance of this distinction will be more apparent when we discuss trouble-shooting your own manuscript.

STAKES

Action by itself can be interesting, even fascinating. For example, a team of skydivers leaping out of a plane is inherently interesting. But what if the skydivers are delivering vaccine to a remote African village threatened by a deadly virus? Now the action takes on more meaning because failure could lead to the death of the villagers. What if the village was the first to be exposed to this extremely deadly, easily communicable virus? Failure to contain and stop the spread of the disease risks spreading it around the world. Now the action takes on even more meaning, because failure could mean worldwide disaster. Imagine that you are one of the skydivers and the village is your hometown, where your mother, father, siblings, spouse, and children all live. Now the risk is personal, so it takes on even more interest. In addition to all of the above, what if you are an epidemiologist who accidentally exposes the village to the virus while conducting research? The whole mess is your fault, and unless you are successful, your family, the village, and everybody else in the world could die.

Jumping out of a plane is interesting action, but knowing the reasons why a character wants to achieve his goal can make it fascinating. The opposite of what is to be gained through success is what is to be risked or lost by failure. Whatever may be gained or lost as a result of a particular effort is known as *stakes*. The more that is at risk and the more personal the consequences, the higher the stakes. All else being equal, the higher the stakes the more interesting the scene.

MOTIVATION

Not everyone with the same objective and stakes will take action to achieve that objective. Think of a crowd witnessing an act of violence. Someone is going to get hurt or even killed if no one takes action, so the stakes are high. The goal of at least some of the witnesses would be to prevent harm to the innocent, but most likely only one person or a few will act to stop the violence. The presence of a goal and stakes is not enough. The missing ingredient comes from within the person, something that compels that person to take action. That something is *motivation*, a need, idea, or emotion that demands that a character take action.[8] The formula for motivation is character + goal + stakes + motivation = action.

ATTEMPT

Once the scene is set up, the character (with a goal, stakes, and motivation) takes some sort of action to achieve his goal. That action may be as simple as picking up a phone, or the action could be dynamic, even violent, such as blowing up a bridge.

Often scenes follow another passage with the same setting, goal, stakes, and motivation, so the beginning of a scene may start with the character acting to achieve his goal. An initial attempt to achieve a goal is a sign that a new scene has begun.

RESISTANCE

Sometimes a character's action to achieve a goal is successful, and if that moves the story forward, so be it. If the character is successful too often, however, the story won't maintain the reader's interest. If the character is so successful that he achieves the story goal, the story is over.

To keep the story interesting, we put obstacles in the character's path. Obstacles can come in many forms, but they have one effect in common: they create resistance to the character's attempt to achieve his goal. An obstacle may complicate, slow, or even block the character's achievement of his objective. Resistance may be from another character, who physically resists the focal character. Resistance may be verbal, as complicated as a legal argument in court or as simple as an opponent saying "No." Resistance may be physical, such as an impassable river, or it may be intangible, such as an equation for nuclear fusion.

CONFLICT

When a motivated character attempting to achieve a goal encounters an obstacle, he tries to eliminate or circumvent the obstacle. He might try to push through resistance; he might try to destroy the obstacle; he might go over, under, or around the obstacle. The character's attempts to overcome an obstacle may be physical, verbal, or mental. A physical, verbal, or mental struggle between opposing forces is called *conflict*.

The formula for conflict is character + goal + stakes + motivation + attempt + resistance = conflict.

TENSION

A character may quickly overcome resistance, he may struggle to overcome resistance over time, or he may fail to overcome the resistance. When a character quickly overcomes resistance, little drama is generated. If a character struggles with resistance or if resistance blocks the character, then an element of uncertainty is created as to whether the goal can be achieved. Anxiety in the mind of the character resulting from uncertainty as to whether the character will overcome an obstacle is referred to as *tension*.

The formula for tension is Conflict +Uncertainty = Tension. For example, Captain Ahab successfully hurls a harpoon into the white whale, but Moby Dick dives below the surface, hiding the effectiveness of the harpoon. Uncertainty about the outcome creates tension in the mind of the character and the reader.

MULTIPLE ATTEMPTS

We don't want our character to achieve his goal too early in the scene, so we often make his first attempt unsuccessful. After the character fails in that attempt, he can't quit because his goal is important and the stakes are high. He must try again. But another obstacle complicates his attempt, resulting in more frustration, more tension, and yet another failure.

Since the character is properly motivated and the stakes are adequate for the situation, he tries to overcome the obstacle yet again. As we saw earlier, easy or too frequent success makes for boring fiction, but having the character try and fail too many times in a row would be monotonous, even exhausting. So how many times should a character attempt to achieve his goal before you either let him succeed or let him fail?

In real life and in fiction, events often occur in sets of three. This phenomenon is sometimes referred to as the "Rule of Three." A scene may include just one attempt or it could include many. When in doubt, try three. For this reason, as you will see later, the proto-type scene includes three attempts.

SUSPENSE

As described above, when a character's attempt is delayed by an obstacle, tension is created in the mind of the character and of the reader. If that uncertainty is drawn out over time, anxiety rises. Uncertainty in the mind of the reader as to whether a character will be successful in achieving his goal over a period of time is called *suspense*. For example, Ahab and his crew wait in their boats for the wounded whale to surface and reveal the outcome of the conflict.

To be effective in generating suspense for the reader, tension must be drawn out in time. Remember, time in fiction is elastic: a second may be described in pages of narrative, while centuries or generations may be compressed into a single sentence.

The formula for suspense is Tension + Time = Suspense. Combining the formulas for conflict, tension, and suspense creates a comprehensive formula for suspense: Character + Goal + Stakes + Motivation + Attempt + Resistance + Uncertainty+ Tension+ Time = Suspense.

CLIMAX

As described in the section about scene setups, the scene is set in some form of crucible that restricts the character's choices. With each of his attempts thus far, the character's choices have narrowed. In the last attempt of the scene, the character encounters another obstacle, and he has only one option left, with no way to avoid it or with no easy exit available. If he fails, he risks losing what is at stake. It's now or never, so the pressure to succeed rises to the boiling point and he exerts maximum effort. That portion of a scene in which conflict and suspense peak prior to resolution is referred to as the *climax*.

RESOLUTION

The climax leads to the scene resolution, which can be either success or failure or some sort of partial success or failure. Since outright success too early or too often in a story lacks drama, the most likely scene resolution is bittersweet success, outright failure, partial failure, or failure that leaves the character even farther from his goals than when the scene started. After the resolution, the scene is over.

In this chapter we have seen that fiction has five elements, that plot has structure on three distinct levels, that fiction-writing has numerous structural units, and that scenes and sequels create an ebb and flow in fiction. We also covered the components of a scene.

In the next chapter we will look at scenes from several different angles.

CHAPTER 2: SCENES, PART II

CHAPTER CONTENTS

- Formula for a scene
- Prototype scene
- Prototype-scene outline
- Benefits of a scene
- Disadvantages of a scene
- Variations in scenes
- Types of scenes

The first chapter shows how scenes work, but that's just the beginning of what we need to create page-turning fiction. Let's build on that knowledge by creating tools that will help us recall the components of scenes in the process of writing. Let's also expand on our knowledge of scenes by looking at their benefits, disadvantages, and variations.

FORMULA

The formula for a scene is Character + Setting + Situation + Crucible + Goal + Stakes + Motivation + Attempt + Resistance + Conflict + Uncertainty + Tension + Time + Suspense + Climax + Resolution = Scene

PROTOTYPE SCENE

We have looked at each part of a scene in detail to gain a thorough understanding of how it works. As an aid to the ongoing use of scenes in day-to-day writing (especially in troubleshooting your own manuscript, as we shall see later) let's look at a *prototype scene*—an ideal, a fully developed model. For your convenience, the components of a scene are shown in italics.

The *scene setup* establishes setting, including time, especially in relation to the previous passage of writing. The setup also establishes the point of view, which in many cases is that of the scene's focal character. The scene setup also establishes the character's *situation*, his predicament. The scene setup, through a combination of situation and setting, establishes a scene *crucible*, the confining circumstances that limit the choices available to the character to deal with his predicament (so the character can't easily walk away from the situation).

The character has a *goal*, the failure of which to achieve would have undesirable consequences, i.e., *stakes*. A goal with stakes helps create character *motivation*.

The character makes an *attempt* to achieve his goal. *Resistance* complicates the character's attempt. This creates *conflict*, which results in *uncertainty* as to whether the character will achieve his goal and *tension* in the mind of the character and the reader.

Since the character is properly motivated and the stakes are adequate, he *attempts* to overcome resistance more than once. Uncertainty about the outcome of the conflict draws out over *time*, creating *suspense* for the reader.

The character tries yet again (his third attempt) to overcome the obstacle. Since the character is confined to the situation somehow by the crucible, and since he has a decreasing number of options and no way out, pressure rises to a breaking point at the scene *climax*.

The outcome of the scene climax is the *resolution*, which may be either success or failure or some variation of either or both. Since outright success too often in the story would be anticlimactic, the more likely scene resolution would be bittersweet success, outright failure, partial failure, or failure that leaves the character even farther from his goals than when the scene started. At the end of the resolution, the scene is over.

PROTOTYPE-SCENE OUTLINE

Let's boil the prototype scene down to its essence, with five easy-to-remember parts.

- Scene setup
- Attempt #1
- Attempt #2
- Attempt #3
- Resolution

BENEFITS OF A SCENE

Scenes offer critical benefits to your writing. As an important structural unit of plot, scenes propel your story forward. Through action and dialogue, the reader learns much about the character. By having the character interact with his surroundings, the reader learns a lot about that setting. Through the character's actions and words during scenes, we glimpse your story's theme. The skill with which you portray scenes is a important expression of your unique writing style.

DISADVANTAGES OF A SCENE

The benefits of scenes are substantial, but scenes may not be the most effective means of developing a character's goals, stakes, and motivation, without which a character's actions may lack sense. Scenes may not be the most effective means of showing a character's thought process or of how and why he selects one particular course of action over another. Scenes move the story forward, which makes them awkward places to share information with your reader.

VARIATIONS IN SCENES

One of the many benefits of writing scenes is their flexibility in meeting the needs of a story. Scenes may be presented in many different ways. They may be lengthened in order to include a character's multiple attempts to achieve a goal. Scenes may be strung together as a *series* of scenes. A scene may be shortened by reducing the number of attempts to just one, or a scene may be truncated by leaving off a portion of it (as when a character's action is interrupted), creating a scene *fragment*. You may eliminate a scene entirely, opting instead to show only a character's reflective response to that event in a sequel.

The prototype scene mentioned above lists specific components in a specified order, but scenes may be presented without all of the prototype parts. Components may be added to those listed in the prototype scene, or the order of scene components may be rearranged.

TYPES OF SCENES

Scenes may be classified by their position within the story (such as an opening scene or a climax scene). A scene may be classified by the fiction-writing mode that dominates its presentation (as in an action scene or a dialogue scene). Some scenes have specialized roles (such as flashback scenes and flashforward scenes). Regardless of where a scene is placed within a story, which fiction-writing mode dominates its presentation, or whether a scene also performs a specialized function, a scene functions much as described above.

In this chapter we have reviewed a formula for a scene, developed a prototype scene, and outlined a skeletal scene. We've examined the benefits of a scene, the disadvantages of a scene, variations in scene presentation, and different types of scenes.

In the next chapter we will analyze an example of a scene.

CHAPTER 3: SCENES, PART III

Here's an example of a scene I wrote for the prologue of a science-fiction novel.

Park Ranger Travis O'Brian braced himself as he held a climbing line snug against his backside. All around him were the forested hills of Yellowstone National Park and the scent of pine. In the distance a ghostlike column of steam rose above the trees, reminding him that Native Americans once viewed the Yellowstone area as a home of evil spirits, a portal to the underworld.

At the other end of the rope, an overweight biologist in blue jeans climbed down a ten-foot rock wall. Nestled in a pear-shaped sinkhole lay an azure-blue pool about five yards wide. Wisps of steam rose from water so clear and deep that it seemed bottomless.

The biologist was there to gather specimens from the water's edge for a research project. O'Brian figured the guy was wasting his time, but it didn't hurt to humor him. "Shoot'n for a Nobel prize or something?"

The curly haired, pug-nosed biologist, Shawn Gruden, flipped up his clip-on sunglasses and laughed. "You never know. The rain forests of the world have yielded new drugs that provide amazing cures. Maybe tucked away in some place like this could be a new species of bacteria or algae that could save the world from suffering."

Right, thought O'Brian, glancing at his watch. If this bozo didn't take too long, he could finish his camp inspections before five o'clock, then stop for a beer on the way home. "What makes you think anything useful could be growing here?"

Gruden reached the edge of the pool and slipped a daypack off his shoulders. "Every microenvironment we've studied has produced plant and animal life unique to its conditions. The more harsh the environment, the more unique have been the adaptations. It's trial-and-error research, but someday I may just get lucky and discover something useful, maybe even a real breakthrough. Apparently the concept is interesting enough for a major pharmaceutical company to fund my research while I prepare a doctoral thesis."

This guy's even more of a nerd than I suspected, thought O'Brian. "I wouldn't think anything could live in hot water."

Gruden had his pack open and its contents spread on the rock around the pool. "You'd be surprised where life can survive, even flourish—from the coldest reaches of the Arctic to the very edge of active volcanoes. I'm hoping that Yellowstone, with all its geysers and hot springs, will yield something exciting."

O'Brian watched silently as Gruden picked up a plastic container that looked like the case for a thermometer. The scientist popped off one end of the container, revealing a plastic stick with a fuzzy end. He leaned over the edge of the pool, exposing his ample butt crack.

O'Brian tightened his grip on the rope, wishing he had run the line around a tree before letting the biologist descend. Rocks around geysers and hot springs tended to be brittle. "Careful now. Letting a scientist get parboiled wouldn't look good in my personnel file."

Gruden sat back on the rock ledge and examined the smudged end of the sample swab. "Not to worry, my friend, not to worry." He slipped the plastic cap back on the swab container and snapped it tight. "One down, and three to go."

The rock under O'Brian shuddered.

"Whoa! What was that?" Gruden edged back from the pool.

"Just a tremor. We get them all the time up here. You know Yellowstone is the site of an ancient volcano, don't you?"

"Supervolcano, actually," said Gruden. "Probably caused an ice age when it erupted."

O'Brian waited a moment, half expecting another tremor. The hair on the back of his neck stood on end. "What do you say we wrap this up and call it a day?"

"Just a few more samples." Gruden snatched up another kit and edged to the pool.

O'Brian pulled the line taut as the biologist leaned close to the steaming water. From deep in the clear-blue pool appeared a dark spot. It blossomed into a billowing black cloud, its edges churning as it expanded. O'Brian pulled hard on the line, yanking Gruden back from the pool.

"Ouch!" screamed Gruden. "What's your problem?"

The black cloud rose quickly, obliterating any trace of blue in the pool. As the blackness reached the surface, the water roiled. O'Brian cringed at the stench of sulfur.

"Crap!" yelled Gruden. "Get me out of here!"

O'Brian pulled with all his strength, hand over hand, hauling Gruden up the wall. As Gruden approached the top of the wall, O'Brian stepped back, dragging the biologist over the edge.

Gruden looked at O'Brian and laughed with relief.

O'Brian panted with exertion, but he couldn't keep himself from chuckling, feeling a little embarrassed.

Another tremor. O'Brian steadied himself.

The rock under them collapsed, cascading with a roar toward the pool.

For a moment, O'Brian felt suspended in mid-air. His stomach seemed to rise within him, like on a roller coaster. His feet caught on rock, and he tumbled end over end toward the pool. His mind flashed bright colors, then all turned black.

Let's analyze this scene by identifying its parts. I'll show the components in capital letters in parentheses.

Park Ranger Travis O'Brian (CHARACTER) braced himself as he held a climbing line snug against his backside. All around him were the forested hills of Yellowstone National Park and the scent of pine. In the distance a ghostlike column of steam rose above the trees, reminding him that native Americans once viewed the Yellowstone area as a home of evil spirits, a portal to the underworld. (SETTING)

At the other end of the rope, an overweight biologist (CHARACTER) in blue jeans climbed down a ten-foot rock wall. Nestled in a pear-shaped sinkhole, lay an azure-blue pool about five yards wide (CRUCIBLE). Wisps of steam rose from water so clear and deep that it seemed bottomless.

The biologist was there to gather specimens from the water's edge for a research project (GOAL). O'Brian figured the guy was wasting his time, but it didn't hurt to humor him. "Shoot'n for a Nobel prize or something?"

The curly haired, pug-nosed biologist, Shawn Gruden, flipped up his clip-on sunglasses and laughed. "You never know. The rain forests of the world have yielded new drugs that provide amazing cures. Maybe tucked away in some place like this could be a new species of bacteria or algae that could save the world from suffering." (STAKES)

Right, thought O'Brian, glancing at his watch. If this bozo didn't take too long, he could finish his camp inspections before five o'clock, then stop for a beer on the way home. (GOAL) "What makes you think anything useful could be growing here?"

Gruden reached the edge of the pool and slipped a daypack off his shoulders. "Every micro-environment we've studied has produced plant and animal life unique to its conditions. The more harsh the environment, the more unique have been the adaptations. It's trial-and-error research, but someday I may just get lucky and discover something useful, maybe even a real breakthrough. Apparently the concept is interesting enough for a major pharmaceutical company to fund my research while I prepare a doctoral thesis." (STAKES)

This guy's even more of a nerd than I suspected, thought O'Brian. "I wouldn't think anything could live in hot water."

Gruden had his pack open and its contents spread on the rock around the pool. "You'd be surprised where life can survive, even flourish—from the coldest reaches of the Arctic to the very edge of active volcanoes. I'm hoping that Yellowstone, with all its geysers and hot springs, will yield something exciting." (STAKES)

O'Brian watched silently as Gruden picked up a plastic container that looked like the case for a thermometer. The scientist popped off one end of the container, revealing a plastic stick with a fuzzy end. He leaned over the edge of the pool, exposing his ample butt crack. (FIRST ATTEMPT)

O'Brian tightened his grip on the rope, wishing he had run the line around a tree before letting the biologist descend. Rocks around geysers and hot springs tended to be brittle. "Careful now. Letting a scientist get parboiled wouldn't look good in my personnel file." (STAKES)

Gruden sat back on the rock ledge and examined the smudged end of the sample swab. "Not to worry, my friend, not to worry." He slipped the plastic cap back on the swab container and snapped it tight. "One down, and three to go." (SUCCESS)

The rock under O'Brian shuddered. (RESISTANCE)

"Whoa! What was that?" Gruden edged back from the pool.

"Just a tremor. We get them all the time up here. You know Yellowstone is the site of an ancient volcano, don't you?" (SITUATION)

"Supervolcano, actually," said Gruden. "Probably caused an ice age when it erupted."

O'Brian waited a moment, half expecting another tremor. The hair on the back of his neck stood on end. "What do you say we wrap this up and call it a day?" (RESISTANCE)

"Just a few more samples." Gruden snatched up another kit and edged to the pool. (SECOND ATTEMPT)

O'Brian pulled the line taut as the biologist leaned close to the steaming water. From deep in the clear-blue pool appeared a dark spot. It blossomed to a billowing black cloud, its edges churning as it expanded. (RESISTANCE) O'Brian pulled hard on the line, yanking Gruden back from the pool. (NEW GOAL: GET OUT!)

"Ouch!" screamed Gruden. "What's your problem?"

The black cloud quickly rose, obliterating any trace of blue in the pool. As the blackness reached the surface, the water roiled. O'Brian cringed at the stench of sulfur.

"Crap!" yelled Gruden. "Get me out of here!"

O'Brian pulled with all his strength, hand over hand, hauling Gruden up the wall. (ATTEMPT) As Gruden approached the top of the wall, O'Brian stepped back, dragging the biologist over the edge. (SUCCESS)

Gruden looked at O'Brian and laughed with relief.

O'Brian panted with exertion, but he couldn't keep himself from chuckling, a little embarrassed.

Another tremor. O'Brian steadied himself. (RESISTANCE and SUCCESS)

The rock under them collapsed, cascading with a roar toward the pool. (RESISTANCE)

For a moment, O'Brian felt suspended in mid-air. His stomach seemed to rise within him, like on a roller coaster. His feet caught on rock, and he tumbled end over end toward the pool. His mind flashed bright colors, then all turned black. (FAILURE)

I drafted this scene prior to starting the manuscript for this book and had no idea I would use it as an example. With that caveat I note that many parts of the prototype scene are present, and they are roughly in the same order as in the prototype scene. Although this scene resembles the prototype scene, it has variations that meet the needs of the story.

Later in this book, I'll show you a technique for troubleshooting your own scenes, but first let's take a detailed look at sequels.

CHAPTER 4: SEQUELS, PART I

CHAPTER CONTENTS

- Components of a sequel
- Formula for a sequel
- Prototype sequel
- Prototype-sequel outline

A sequel mimics real life. When something important happens, we tend to respond first with emotion. After our emotions settle down we try to make sense of our circumstances, reviewing recent events, evaluating how the new situation affects us, formulating alternative courses of action, and planning our next move. After forming a judgment, we make a decision about what to do next. To more fully understand a sequel, let's look at its components.

SETUP

As does a scene, a sequel may need a setup to establish time, place, viewpoint character, and situation. A setup may be quite long, or it may be as short as a line or two. Often, though, a sequel immediately follows the scene that preceded it and needs no setup.

CHARACTER

A scene focuses on the character attempting to achieve a goal, but the subsequent sequel may feature another character. For example, a scene in *Moby-Dick* shows Captain Ahab nailing a gold coin to the ship's mast as he rallies his crew to help him find the great white whale. The subsequent sequel features Ishmael as he wonders just what he has signed on for. Almost all sequels feature the focal character of the previous scene, but if the focal character of a scene is not the viewpoint character, the subsequent sequel will most likely feature the viewpoint character.

EMOTION

The resolution of a scene shapes the character's emotional reaction. A scene may end with the achievement of the character's short-term goal. A scene may end with outright failure or, even worse, as when the character ends up farther from his objective than when he started. Also, a scene may end with some combination of success and failure, such as partial success. The character's emotional reaction may therefore range anywhere from euphoria to devastation.

In fiction as in real life, reaction to a major event may include multiple emotions, possibly a chaotic mixture of feelings. Imagine you just won the lottery for a hundred million dollars. Your first reaction would likely include disbelief mixed with euphoria, followed by excitement about being wealthy and able to fulfill your wildest fantasies. You might feel benevolent now that you can help the less fortunate by sharing your money. Smugness might creep into your feelings as you realize that those bums who thought you would never amount to anything will now have to look at you differently. Horror that you might owe the government a huge chunk of your newfound cash could also manifest itself as greed. Sadness might overtake all of your other feelings as you realize that your relationship with friends and family might be forever changed. The potential loss of privacy or even the threat of personal harm may accompany your new wealth, leading to dread and fear.

Now imagine the mix of emotions you might experience if you had just been convicted of a horrible crime and sentenced to death. Sequels provide you with the opportunity to portray any emotion or combination of feelings you choose.

The intensity of emotional reaction may range from almost nothing to mental paralysis. A scene ending that generates no feelings in the character may also fail to generate an emotional response from the reader. Lack of emotion may be an intentional device used to portray a particularly tough-minded character, such as an assassin. Our goal as fiction writers is to generate emotion in our readers, so we want scene endings to be significant, often dramatic enough to paralyze our character with emotion, possibly chaotic emotion that forces the character to grapple with his feelings.

THOUGHT

At some point after a significant event, our emotions subside, and we begin to think. As stated by Jack M. Bickham in *Scene & Structure* (1993), "At first this thought may be somewhat haphazard and confused by emotion . . . ," but sooner or later the character begins to think rationally. Bickham identified three phases in the thought process of sequels: (1) review, (2) analysis, and (3) planning.[9]

REVIEW

The character looks back on the scene and remembers the outcome. For example, after an athlete literally or figuratively drops the ball, he may replay the failure in his mind. The review phase is likely to employ the fiction-writing mode of recollection. Occasionally the review may include a flashback, where the character relives a scene as if were happening in real time.

ANALYSIS

Just as in real life after a significant occurrence, at some point we switch from reviewing events to evaluating our new situation, the meaning of everything that has happened.[10] The character might recall his goal for the scene, how it was to help achieve his overall objective, and how the scene resolution hinders or helps him achieve the goal. For example, the athlete who dropped the ball might realize that his failure made it more difficult for his team to win the game and eventually qualify for the championship.

PLANNING

At some point the character begins to think ahead about how he can either (1) chart a new course of action to achieve his goal or (2) select a new short-term goal. In real life we try to make decisions rationally and logically, and so should your character. To make this process believable, especially if the story is approaching a key turning point, show the character's chain of thought.

The character might consider options, weigh the merits of each, discard some, and rank the rest. The situation may involve equally unsatisfactory alternatives, making the whole process a gut-wrenching dilemma. Eventually, the character lays out a plan for struggling forward, a new path to his achieving his overall objective.

DECISION

All that remains of the sequel is for the character to make a decision about his new short-term goal. A character caught on the horns of a dilemma may have an epiphany that shows him the way forward. Once a character whittles his choices down to his best choice, he may experience a flashforward that allows him to visualize his path to success. He may agonize over the decision, considering it from all angles and weighing the risks, or he might rush to judgment, but once he decides what to do, the sequel is over. For example, a basketball player, after weighing options for his next move, decides to take a long shot to score three points.

NEW SCENE

The moment the character takes action to achieve his new goal, a new scene begins. Remember, the definition of a *scene* is a passage of writing in which the character attempts to achieve a goal. The character might take dramatic action to begin a new scene (such as firing a pistol), or the action could be moderate, such as thumbing the safety lever of a handgun to the "off" position, or as subtle as moving his hand closer to his holster.

FORMULA

The formula for a prototype sequel: Character + Emotion + Review + Analysis + Planning + Decision = Sequel.

PROTOTYPE SEQUEL

We have looked at each part of a sequel in detail to gain a thorough understanding of how it works. As an aid to the ongoing use of sequels in day-to-day writing (especially in troubleshooting your own manuscript, as we shall see later), let's look at a *prototype sequel*—an ideal, a fully developed model. For your convenience, the components of a sequel are shown in italics.

The resolution of the preceding scene left the character in a state of *emotion*. As the character gains control of his feelings, he begins to *think*, to reason through the situation. In the process, the main character *reviews* recent events, *analyzes* the situation, and *plans*. Once the character has selected a course of action, he makes a *decision* to act, which marks the end of the sequel.

PROTOTYPE-SEQUEL OUTLINE

Expressed in the form of an outline, a sequel looks like this.

- Emotion

- Review

- Analysis

- Planning

- Decision

In this chapter we have examined the components of a sequel, a formula for a sequel, a prototype sequel, and a prototype sequel outline. In the next chapter we look at the benefits and disadvantages of sequels.

CHAPTER 5: SEQUELS, PART II

In this chapter we will examine the benefits and disadvantages of sequels.

- Goals
- Characterization
- Exposition
- Pace
- Summarization
- Transition
- Flashback and flashforward
- Epiphany
- Foreshadowing
- Reader involvement
- Disadvantages

GOALS

Fiction is built upon suspension of disbelief, so irrational behavior by the focal character risks shattering that illusion. Readers insist that a character have a reason for his actions—that it makes sense for the character to strive for a particular goal.

The number-one purpose of a sequel is to justify the character's next course of action, to bridge the gap between one scene's resolution and the next scene's direction. You may write great scenes, but the reader isn't likely to tolerate a character who impulsively leaps from one short-term goal to another.

Scenes dramatize conflict, but conflict for conflict's sake isn't enough.[11] The more a plot twists and turns, the more those changes require explanation to make them believable. At the micro level, plot consists of cause and effect: a new goal or course of action (effect) requires development (cause) to show how it emerged. If a character's action "just happens," it won't seem plausible.

A sequel follows the character's chain of logic, his pattern of rationalization, showing that his decision is a product of intelligence and reasoning. Sequels link scenes by showing how a character gets from one point to another—both mentally and physically.

A classic scene is the one where a detective's only clue turns out to be a dead end. The subsequent sequel may show his frustration, his analysis of the situation, his planning, and his decision. The sequel builds a bridge from the dead end to a new course of investigation.

CHARACTERIZATION

The first phase of a sequel allows you to show the character's temperament, his emotions, and how he demonstrates them. A character's reaction may range from little or no emotion to such an extreme emotion that his behavior borders on the irrational. The type of emotion demonstrated by a character tells you a lot about his personality. How does your character react to success? With humility or with bravado? How does he handle failure? With quiet resolve or with anger? What does that tell you about your character's personality?

The thinking phase of a sequel allows you to show how the character's mind works. Sequels often show a character caught on the horns of a *dilemma*: a situation involving a choice between equally unsatisfactory alternatives.[12] What is the character's thought process? Does the character make snap judgments, or does he consider the situation from all angles? How does the character make sense of complex problems? Does he think deftly or clumsily? How does the character work out an answer?[13] What better way to understand a character than by learning how his mind works?

The final phase of a sequel is the decision. How does your character make a decision? Does he procrastinate? Brood? Agonize? Forge ahead? Does the character second-guess himself? Worry? Does he have nagging doubts? Does the character take fate into his own hands, or does he wimp out? What does that tell you about his personality?

As you can see, the emotion, thinking, and decision phases of a sequel provide powerful tools to use for character development.

EXPOSITION

In my book *Fiction-Writing Modes: Eleven essential tools for bringing your fiction to life*, *exposition* is the mode for conveying information. Exposition may be delivered through three methods:

- Narrative exposition (where the all-knowing, invisible narrator simply states it)
- Expository devices (treasure maps, diaries, newspaper clippings, etc.)
- Characters (by what they say, hear, see, smell, feel, think, or recall)

Each of these techniques has advantages and disadvantages, and each requires skillful presentation for effective use.

One of the most effective ways to present information through a character is including it in the thinking phase of a sequel. The character is already in thought as he reviews recent events, analyzes the situation, considers his options, and begins to develop a plan.

Information may surface in a sequel through various channels. The character may simply recall information from the recesses of his mind. Information may be revealed through a flashback scene, where the character relives a significant moment of his past. Other characters may provide information through dialogue if that part of the sequel is related verbally.

We tend to remember information best when it is steeped in emotion (Can you remember your first kiss?), and since a sequel begins with emotion, it is a particularly effective place to convey information.

The right time to present information is when the reader most needs it. What better time to share information than when the character reviews events, analyzes his situation, or plans his next move?

The amount of exposition that can be effectively presented in sequels is limited only by the needs of the story and the imagination of the author. Think of the massive amount of information revealed by Dan Brown in his hugely successful novel *The Da Vinci Code*.

PACE

Scenes, by their nature, tend to be fast-paced and full of conflict, tension, and suspense. Sequels are full of emotion, reflection, and thinking, so they tend to be slower than scenes. Writing with both scenes and sequels creates the opportunity to manage the tempo of your story.

The progression of a story is sometimes represented graphically by a saw-tooth pattern. Scenes represent the upward slopes, while sequels are the downward slopes. Presenting scene after scene can wear down your character and your reader. Interspersing sequels among the scenes provides a contrast in pace and gives your reader a break from the intensity. Skillful placement of sequels allows you to control the rhythm and pace of your story.

Even in the most intense thrillers, the character needs to rest now and then to lick his wounds, to figure out what hit him, to develop a new game plan. For example, when your hero fights off one bad guy after another, you can show him taking a break to reload, figure out who betrayed him, or devise an escape plan.

SUMMARIZATION

Scenes are presented in the "now" of the story, showing events in real time, as they occur. Sequels, with their emphasis on thinking and analysis, offer opportunities to recap events. What better time to summarize an event than when the character is reviewing events or analyzing his situation?

For example, if you want to summarize an argument between two lovers without actually portraying the event in real-time detail, write a sequel starting with the focal character's emotional reaction to the fight, then in the thinking phase summarize the fight before moving on to the character's planning of his next move.

TRANSITION

Sequels connect scenes to one another, so it is natural to consider sequels as a form of transition, and they are. We have seen that sequels can help a character transition to the next goal, but sequels can also facilitate changes in location and time.

Scenes tend to be largely located in one setting during a short period of time. Sequels have more flexibility with location and time. A sequel can span seconds, months, or years. In a sequel a character can sit tight or he can move around as much as needed. Consider the following sequel.

Hal's betrayal hit Georgia like a punch in the gut. She slumped onto the couch and crushed a pillow to her chest.

How could she have misjudged him? And how could he have been so cruel? Would she ever be able to show her face in public again? Would she ever be able to trust a man? The pain and humiliation would scar her forever.

But was she going to let that bastard ruin her life? Hell no. She wouldn't let that son of a bitch slow her down, not even for a day. She'd call Paige and Katrina. Tonight they'd put on their steamiest outfits and set the town on fire.

The sequel above takes place in one location and consumes only a little story time. Compare it to the following.

Hal's betrayal hit Georgia like a punch in the gut. She locked herself in her apartment for the night. The next day she booked a cabin on the longest cruise she could find.

Over the coming weeks she sailed around the world, wondering how she could have misjudged him.

And how could the man she loved be so cruel? She doubted she could ever return to Memphis and show her face in public. She'd never trust another man. The pain and humiliation would scar her for life. When the cruise was over, she packed her belongings and moved back home with her parents in San Francisco.

Years later she began to wonder why she was letting that bastard, Hal, ruin her life. Over the coming months she began to realize that she needed to take charge of her own life. Maybe she should get her hair done and buy a steamy new outfit. She'd call a friend, and they would set the town on fire.

Where each phase of a scene tends to be tightly focused in time and place, each phase of a sequel (emotion, thinking, and decision) can be spread widely over time and space to fit the needs of the story.

FLASHBACK AND FLASHFORWARD

Sequels are natural launching pads for flashbacks and flash-forwards. What better time for a character to let his mind relive a significant past event (a *flashback*) than when he is thinking about his current predicament? Here's an example of a flashback situation:

A teenager has just experienced an obstacle that frustrates his plans to attain a goal. He reacts emotionally to the event and begins to review the circumstances that led up to it. He may enter the phase of analysis, where he considers his current situation. He sees no way forward, and in his discouragement he is reminded of some significant event in his past. His mind slips into a vivid, in-the-moment reenactment of that event (a flashback). After his thoughts return to the present, he realizes that the relived event has provided him with a clue or a course action for getting out of his current predicament.

When a character considers a potential new course of action, what better time for him to slip into a *flashforward* where he imagines that action or its outcome in detail as if it were already reality? For example:

A character is well into a sequel, and he has narrowed his potential courses of action to one. As he hesitates before making the decision, he visualizes his course of action vividly as it will happen. He may even imagine in detail his euphoria, acts of celebration, and the congratulatory remarks of others. After the character's thoughts return to the present, he makes his decision with greater confidence.

A flashforward provides an opportunity to present dramatically a scene that *won't* materialize in the real time of the story. The character and the reader get the benefit of experiencing the scene, but the course of action eventually fails to happen as visualized, and the character's hopes are dashed again.

Examples of flashbacks in published fiction abound. For example, *Hatchet* by Gary Paulsen has many flashbacks as the protagonist relives the events related to his parents' divorce. Flashforwards are not so common, but John Grisham uses one in *The Client*[14], where an attorney imagines the harsh treatment that may be in store for her young client. The next time you notice a flashback or a flashforward in published fiction, take note of whether the character is engaged in reflection, quite probably after an emotional experience (i.e., in a sequel).

EPIPHANY

The thinking phase of a sequel is also a logical place for your character to experience an *epiphany*, that burst of insight that provides him with an opportunity to move ahead. For example:

Your character is devastated by her loss of several patients to a deadly virus. To no avail, she has racked her brain to think of a successful treatment for the disease. Her mind wanders, and she finds herself focusing on some seemingly irrelevant image or recollection. A light within her suddenly clicks on when she recognizes a relationship between her problem and the seemingly irrelevant. A solution presents itself.

If the sequel includes either a flashback or a flashforward, a great place for an epiphany is immediately afterward. For example:

In the thinking phase of your sequel, the character vaguely recalls his high-school football coach saying, "What you can visualize, you can do." Your character's thoughts slip back to that time, and he relives that moment as if it were happening all over again. Your character's thoughts return to the present, and he goes about his business. A burst of insight (epiphany) shows him that the flashback has helped him see a new course of action.

FORESHADOWING

Sequels may foreshadow events to come. In Orson Scott Card's *Ender's Game*, most of the chapters begin with a section in italics. Many of those sections are sequels portraying adult reactions to events surrounding the main character, Ender Wiggin. Some of those sequels foreshadow what lies ahead for Ender.[15]

READER INVOLVEMENT

Sequels can deepen satisfaction with the story by allowing your reader to share more than the physical aspects of the character's journey. Each phase of a sequel can enrich your reader's experience.

In the emotion phase of a sequel, the reader can suffer, worry, or celebrate alongside the character as he experiences emotions ranging anywhere from devastation to euphoria. In the review phase of a sequel, the reader is reminded of what happened in the past and why it is important.[16] In the analysis phase the reader gets to see how the character's mind works as he studies his new situation. One of the character's alternative courses of action is to quit, so this phase provides an opportunity to let the reader feel that temptation and to understand why your character can't give up.[17]

The last phase of a sequel allows you to share with the reader your character's decision-making process. This allows the reader to understand the decision, whether or not he agrees with the character's choice. Showing the character's logic, even if it's irrational, builds believability and helps you hook the reader and pull him into the story.[18]

DISADVANTAGES OF SEQUELS

One of the benefits of sequels is that they provide a breather for the character and the reader. Therein also lies the greatest disadvantage of sequels: they slow the pace of the story. Each of the benefits of sequels also presents a potential disadvantage if presented in a manner that bogs down the story.

In this chapter we examined the many benefits of a sequel and its disadvantages. In the next chapter we will explore variations in the way sequels can be presented.

CHAPTER 6: SEQUELS, PART III

In this chapter we will examine variations in the way to present sequels.

- Skipping sequels
- Complete sequels
- Lengthen sequels
- Shorten sequels
- Interrupt sequels
- Change the order of sequel components
- Shredded sequels
- Delay sequels
- Prequels
- Sequels in genre fiction

VARIATIONS IN SEQUELS

One of the many benefits of writing sequels is their flexibility in meeting the needs of a story. The following sections explain the choices available.

SKIPPING SEQUELS

Every scene has a sequel. In real life we can't avoid this phenomenon. After an important event we always react internally in some way. That reaction may be prolonged, or it may consume only a moment. The reaction may be pronounced, or it may be subtle. In fiction, our characters also react internally to an important event. Just because an internalization occurs, however, doesn't mean that we, as authors, must portray that reaction in our writing.

Skipping sequels is a common technique. In each of the novels I analyzed, the number of scenes far surpassed the number of sequels shown. The most frequent variation regarding sequels is to not show the sequel. You can skip writing a sequel simply by starting a new scene rather than showing the character's reflective reaction.

Does this mean that sequels are unimportant? Not at all. Just because a carpenter doesn't use a hammer for every task doesn't mean the hammer isn't a valuable tool.

Given the substantial advantages of writing sequels, why would you skip them? Reasons abound for omitting a sequel, and those reasons mirror the benefits of sequels: goals, characterization, exposition, summarization, transition, and reader involvement.

The number-one role of sequels is to justify the character's next move by revealing his rationale for setting a new goal or new course. If the character's next move is obvious or if the new course can be justified in another way, then showing the character's decision-making process isn't necessary. The more linear the storyline, the less important it is to show a sequel. When action is fast-paced, as in presenting a sequence of scenes one right after another, or if the character is under intense time pressure, slowing the pace to present a sequel could seem cumbersome, even absurd.

Sequels offer an opportunity to develop character, to show your character's emotions, how he thinks, and how he makes a decision. But sequels are not the only means of developing character. As authors we have other tools to use for characterization, including action and dialogue. In some stories, such as those in many thrillers, the main character needs to come across as coolheaded and decisive, so spending a lot of time showing the character's emotions, his reasoning, and his decision-making process might be counterproductive. In a series of novels, the character's personality doesn't change much, if at all, from book to book, so the characterization benefits of sequels may not be needed and may actually get in the way.

Sequels offer an opportunity to share information, but sequels are not the only way to use exposition. Information may also be delivered through dialogue or expository devices. Information may be presented through the viewpoint character during a scene.

Many of the novels I analyzed simply presented information directly from the narrator as a passage of narrative-exposition.

Likewise for summarization. Sequels are a convenient mechanism for summarizing events, especially in the review phase, but summary can also be delivered directly from the narrator as a passage of narrative-summarization.

Sequels can be an effective means of transition between scenes, but a transition can be accomplished by using various other means. Furthermore, when one scene follows another with little change in time, place, and viewpoint, then very little transition may be needed.

Sequels provide an opportunity to enhance reader involvement, but so do scenes. Action and dialogue (the backbone of scenes) can generate lots of reader involvement.

Your decision to write a sequel or to skip it can, and should, be dictated by the needs of the story. That decision also reflects your unique writing style. But your decision isn't limited to a simple choice of writing a sequel or not, because sequels may be presented in a number of ways, each one offering advantages.

I won't provide a specific example of a skipped sequel, because they are quite common. Every novel I analyzed had numerous examples of two or more sequential scenes without the presentation of an intervening sequel.

COMPLETE SEQUELS

The opposite of skipping a sequel is to write a full-blown sequel, one that resembles the prototype sequel described earlier. The benefits of writing sequels were outlined earlier in this chapter, so I won't repeat them.

A complete sequel may be exactly what the story needs. Some writing situations almost demand a sequel. The more twists, turns, surprises, and revelations in a story, the more critical it is to show the corresponding sequels. The more emotionally devastating the previous scene ending, the more the need for a sequel.[19]

The bigger the change in direction from one scene to another, the greater the need for a sequel to explain the change. A scene that stops a character in his tracks (as when he reaches a dead end) probably needs a sequel to get the character moving again.

Fully developed sequels that resemble the prototype were relatively few in the novels I analyzed, but most had at least a couple of them. Examples of such sequels are in *One for the Money* by Janet Evanovich[20], *The Client* by John Grisham[21], and *Ender's Game* by Orson Scott Card.[22]

If novelists often skip sequels and full-fledged sequels are relatively few, how are authors using the benefits of sequels to meet the needs of the story? The answer lies in the many other variations of sequel presentation.

LENGTHEN SEQUELS

A sequel may be lengthened by expanding any of its components or by adding new components. Each phase of a sequel (setup, emotion, review, analysis, planning, and decision) may be amplified out of proportion to the others.[23] Scenes require tight, moment-by-moment development[24] for effective presentation, but you have more flexibility with sequels, which may be loosely organized around the ever-changing feelings and thoughts of the character.[25] For example, Nicholas Sparks expands sequels to comprise entire chapters in *The Lucky One*.[26]

Sequels may be expanded by interrupting the character's thoughts with segments of dialogue or incidental action. In *The Lucky One*, Sparks interrupts a chapter-long sequel to insert a conversation, then returns to the sequel to finish the chapter.[27]

SHORTEN SEQUELS

A sequel may be shortened in two ways. It may be compressed by collapsing[28] each part into the fewest possible words.[29]

Here's an example of a compressed sequel, with the components shown in parentheses.

> Damn! (emotion) How did that happen? (review) This is a mess. How can I fix this? (analysis) Should I do this, that, or just give up? (planning) What the heck, when in doubt, "Charge!" (decision)

A sequel may be shortened by leaving out parts. For example, if the setting and situation are evident from the previous passage, no setup may be necessary. Any part of a sequel may be left out.

Each of the novels I analyzed had a number of examples of shortened sequels. Next to omitting a sequel, shortening a sequel is the most common variation.

INTERRUPT SEQUELS

Rather than showing a sequel in its entirety, you may interrupt the sequel with a new scene, [30] leaving an incomplete passage, more specifically a *sequel fragment*. Reasons for interrupting a sequel include (1) to increase the pace of the story, (2) to prevent the character from figuring out what to do next, and (3) to increase the reader's anxiety. You have the option of showing the remainder of the unfinished sequel later if you so choose.

Sequels may be interrupted with either complete scenes or scene fragments. As previously discussed, sequels may be interrupted with remembered scenes, also known as *flashbacks*, or a sequel may be interrupted with an imagined scene, also known as a *flashforward*.

CHANGE THE ORDER OF SEQUEL COMPONENTS

The prototype sequel lists components in logical order, but the order of scene components may be rearranged[31] to fit the needs of the story. For example, your story may show a character rushing to a judgment or making a snap decision, then changing his mind and starting all over again.

SHREDDED SEQUELS

Sequels may be chopped to bits and sprinkled throughout the subsequent scene by using what I call *shredded sequels*. This technique may be useful in thrillers and other fast-paced fiction where the presentation of a fully developed sequel risks slowing the pace. Another reason for presenting sequels in shredded form is to show the character as being decisive, working to achieve his new goal, then reflecting on the decision already made and how he made that decision.

DELAYED SEQUELS

Instead of showing a sequel immediately after the corresponding scene, you may show the sequel later in the story, where the information is more interesting. Early in Stephenie Meyer's *Twilight*, Edward Cullen has a powerful reaction to the new girl in school.[32] Not until halfway through the book do we see Cullen's reaction in the form of a sequel.[33]

PREQUELS

If we can delay a sequel and show it later than its traditional position immediately after a scene ending, then why can't we place a sequel *before* the scene, as a *prequel*? The answer is that we can. For example, in *Twilight*, Stephenie Meyer uses a sequel in her preface, where the main character reflects on her predicament by thinking, "I'd never given much thought to how I would die . . ."[34] The scene that precedes this sequel doesn't appear until the end of the story, in the climax.[35]

SEQUELS IN GENRE FICTION

The treatment of sequels varies with the respective genre. In general, romance novels are more likely to utilize sequels than thrillers. But once again, the use of sequels varies with the needs of the story and with the style of the author. Janet Evanovich, in *One for the Money,* is relatively stingy with sequels, opting to focus on action, while Dan Brown, in *The Da Vinci Code,* uses sequels extensively to show the main character sorting through information and clues.

Nicholas Sparks, in *The Lucky One*, uses sequels a lot to show the motivation of the villain. Stephenie Meyer, in *Twilight*, also a love story, uses sequels sparingly. After all, sequels focus on the thoughts of the viewpoint character, and a young woman dating a vampire is clearly not thinking rationally.

In this chapter we have examined variations in how you may present sequels. In the next chapter we'll take a look at examples of sequels.

CHAPTER 7: SEQUELS, PART IV

EXAMPLE OF A SEQUEL

In Chapter 3 we examined a scene about a park ranger and a biologist in Yellowstone National Park. Let's continue with that story to see examples of ways you can use sequels.

O'Brian woke to another tremor, his head throbbing. He coughed at the stink of sulfur. He ached all over, but nothing seemed broken. Remembering the fall, he staggered to his feet.

Broken rocks lay in a pile against the wall, and he figured he could climb out easily. His hand brushed against the climbing line. "Gruden! You all right?"

The steaming pool of black water rumbled as it boiled.

O'Brian tugged on the line, and it yielded without resistance. He pulled again until he saw that the line led into the dark pool.

"No!" he screamed, his mind nearly exploding. He planted his boots on solid rock and pulled hard. Several feet of line drew close, but then it drew tight.

He pulled with all his strength. The line wouldn't budge.

Recalling how he could unsnag a fishing line, he sidled a few feet to the left, then pulled again. Still nothing.

He raced to the right and tried again. The line held tight.

Releasing some slack, he ran to the other side of the pool. He yanked on the line, then let out some rope. The line pulled taut then drew away from him, as if it was weighted. O'Brian pulled hard, hand over hand, hauling the line in as fast as he could.

Finally, out of the black, boiling water bobbed the body of the biologist. With a burst of strength, O'Brian heaved the line back, dragging the body onto the rocky edge of the pool.

O'Brian paused, staring at the biologist's back as the body lay on its side. The skin on Gruden's arm bubbled with blisters. For a moment O'Brian imagined being boiled alive. He hoped Gruden had drowned quickly.

Once the initial shock wore off, O'Brian wondered what he should do next. There was no way that the biologist could still be alive, but he felt he should check for vital signs. That would be the professional thing to do.

He gently clutched Gruden's wrist, but then recoiled at the heat radiating from the steaming flesh. He took a breath, then eased his hand around the wrist to see if he could detect a pulse.

As his hand closed around the wrist, another tremor rocked the ledge, and O'Brian lost his balance. Reflexively, he tightened his grip to keep from falling over the body. As he did, the flesh of Gruden's lower arm slid away from the underlying bone.

O'Brian sat in the late-afternoon shade against the wall of the sinkhole, grateful that a breeze diluted some of the sulfur stench.

Sheriff Barnhouse, a beefy man with thick eyebrows and a western-style hat, sat on a rock nearby. "Start from the beginning and tell me exactly what happened."

Radios squawked as a couple of EMS technicians finished examining Gruden's body at the edge of the black, bubbling pool.

As O'Brian described the events of the afternoon, the sheriff scribbled in a notebook. One of the EMS techs, a lanky blonde named Hightower, unzipped an empty body bag. The other tech, a stout Hispanic named Lopez, helped her spread the bag next to Gruden. Together, they eased the body onto the open bag.

The blonde packed various supplies back into cases, while Lopez pulled the sides of the body bag together and tugged on the zipper.

O'Brian forced himself to look at Gruden's red, blistered face one last time, figuring he owed the man at least a silent farewell.

What O'Brian saw next caused him to shoot to his feet. "Hold it!"

The sheriff nearly dropped his notebook, and reached for his sidearm. The EMS techs froze.

O'Brian hesitated. What he was about to say would sound crazy. He had to say it anyway. "I think I saw his eyes open."

As we did in Chapter 3, let's analyze the story. I'll label the components in all caps and enclose them in parentheses.

O'Brian woke to another tremor, his head throbbing. He coughed at the stink of sulfur. He ached all over, but nothing seemed broken. Remembering the fall, he staggered to his feet. (SETUP)

Broken rocks lay in a pile against the wall, and he figured he could climb out easily. (ANALYSIS OF SITUATION) His hand brushed against the climbing line. "Gruden! You all right?" (REVIEW OF EVENTS AND CONTINUED ANALYSIS OF SITUATION)

The steaming pool of black water rumbled as it boiled.

O'Brian tugged on the line, and it yielded without resistance. He pulled again until he saw that the line led into the dark pool. (HERE THE SEQUEL IS CUT OFF BY NEW INFORMATION

THAT DEMANDS ACTION IN THE FORM OF A
NEW SCENE)

"No!" he screamed, his mind nearly exploding.
He planted his boots on solid rock and pulled hard.
(NEW GOAL AND ATTEMPT TO ACHIEVE IT)
Several feet of line drew close, but then it drew tight.

He pulled with all his strength. The line wouldn't
budge. (RESISTANCE)

Recalling how he could unsnag a fishing line,
he sidled a few feet to the left, then pulled again.
(SECOND ATTEMPT) Still nothing. (RESISTANCE)

He raced to the right and tried again. The line
held tight. (THIRD ATTEMPT)

Releasing some slack, he ran to the other side
of the pool. He yanked on the line, then let out some
rope. (FOURTH ATTEMPT) The line pulled taut
then drew away from him, as if it was weighted.
O'Brian pulled hard, hand over hand, hauling the
line in as fast as he could.

Finally, out of the black, boiling water bobbed
the body of the biologist. With a burst of strength,
O'Brian heaved the line back, dragging the body onto

the rocky edge of the pool. (SUCCESS MARKS THE END OF THE SCENE)

O'Brian paused, staring at the biologist's back as the body lay on its side. The skin on Gruden's arm bubbled with blisters. For a moment O'Brian imagined being boiled alive. He hoped Gruden had drowned quickly. (NEW SEQUEL, ANALYSIS OF SITUATION)

Once the initial shock wore off, O'Brian wondered what he should do next. (THINKING) There was no way that the biologist could still be alive, but he felt he should check for vital signs. (POSSIBLE COURSE OF ACTION) That would be the professional thing to do. (DECISION)

He gently clutched Gruden's wrist, but then recoiled at the heat radiating from the steaming flesh. (NEW SCENE: FIRST ATTEMPT AND RESISTANCE) He took a breath, then eased his hand around the wrist to see if he could detect a pulse. (SECOND ATTEMPT)

As his hand closed around the wrist, another tremor rocked the ledge, and O'Brian lost his balance. Reflexively, he tightened his grip to keep from falling over the body. As he did, the flesh of Gruden's lower arm slid away from the underlying bone. (DISASTER MARKS THE END OF THE SCENE

O'Brian sat in the late-afternoon shade against the wall of the sinkhole, grateful that a breeze diluted some of the sulfur stench. (SEQUEL SETUP)

Sheriff Barnhouse, a beefy man with thick eyebrows and a western-style hat, sat on a rock nearby. "Start from the beginning and tell me exactly what happened." (REVIEW)

Radios squawked as a couple of EMS technicians finished examining Gruden's body at the edge of the black, bubbling pool. (ANALYSIS OF SITUATION)

As O'Brian described the events of the afternoon, the sheriff scribbled in a notebook. (REVIEW) One of the EMS techs, a lanky blonde named Hightower, unzipped an empty body bag. The other tech, a stout Hispanic named Lopez, helped her spread the bag next to Gruden. Together, they eased the body onto the open bag.

The blonde packed various supplies back into cases, while Lopez pulled the sides of the body bag together and tugged on the zipper.

O'Brian forced himself to look at Gruden's red, blistered face one last time, figuring he owed the man at least a silent farewell. (DECISION)

What O'Brian saw next caused him to shoot to his feet. "Hold it!"

(THE SEQUEL IS CUT SHORT BY A NEW DEVELOPMENT THAT DEMANDS IMMEDIATE ACTION IN THE FORM OF A NEW SCENE)

This excerpt provides two examples of sequels in a manuscript. Neither sequel conforms to the prototype sequel, but they do show how sequels can be varied to fit the needs of the story.

In the next chapter we'll take a look at passages of writing that are neither scenes nor sequels.

CHAPTER 8: OTHER PASSAGES OF WRITING

CHAPTER CONTENTS

- Passages of interiority
- Passages of exteriority
- Passages of conversation
- Passages of activity
- Passages with unclear purpose
- Problem-solving passages

So far, the only passages of writing we have addressed are scenes and sequels. In the real world of fiction, from a rough draft to a published novel, passages of writing may be classified into four groups: (1) scenes, (2) sequels, (3) passages that are *neither* scenes nor sequels, and (4) passages that include elements of *both* scenes and sequels.

NEITHER SCENES NOR SEQUELS

I've defined a *scene* as a passage of writing in which a character attempts to achieve a goal. A *sequel* is a passage of writing in which a character has a reflective response to the resolution of a scene. Passages that are neither scenes nor sequels may be divided into four groups based upon their most prominent fiction-writing mode:

1. Passages of interiority: recollection, introspection, sensation, emotion
2. Passages of exteriority: description, exposition, narration, and transition
3. Passages of conversation: dialogue or monologue
4. Passages of activity: action and summarization

PASSAGES OF INTERIORITY

Passages of introspection, sensation, emotion, or recollection in which the character is neither attempting to achieve a goal nor reacting reflectively to what happened to him in a previous scene are neither sequels nor scenes. Such passages may serve a need perceived by the author, or they may have little value at all. In such passages, nothing seems to happen, because, well, nothing much *is* happening. A classic example is the entire first chapter Herman Melville's *Moby-Dick*.[36]

PASSAGES OF EXTERIORITY

Passages narrated directly to the reader (exteriority) with no attempt to disguise the words as being filtered through the consciousness of a viewpoint character were common in most of the novels I studied. Usually, the narrative combined with other fiction-writing modes to create a passage of narrative-description, narrative-exposition, or narrative-transition. Such passages are frequently found near the beginning of a chapter as a way to set up a scene. Examples of narrative-summary appear in Gary Paulsen's *Hatchet*.[37] An example of narrative-exposition may be found on the first page of John Grisham's *The Client*.[38] In addition to narration, these passages frequently include description, exposition, transition, and summarization, as did Michael Crichton in *Jurassic Park*.[39]

PASSAGES OF CONVERSATION

Passages of dialogue or monologue in which the character is not attempting to achieve a goal nor reacting reflectively to a scene are neither sequels nor scenes. An extreme example is Chapter XL of

Moby-Dick, where Melville portrays the crew of the *Pequod* on deck singing and talking.[40]

PASSAGES OF ACTIVITY

Passages of action or summarization in which the character is not attempting to achieve a goal nor reacting reflectively to a scene are neither sequels nor scenes. Chapter II of *Charlotte's Web,* by E. B. White, includes lots of activity, but much of it is neither a scene nor a sequel.[41]

Passages that are neither scenes nor sequels are easy to identify. They're usually the parts of a book you're tempted to skip.

BOTH SCENES AND SEQUELS

Passages that include elements of both scenes and sequels may be divided into two types: (1) passages with an unclear purpose, and (2) problem-solving passages.

PASSAGES WITH UNCLEAR PURPOSE

As I analyzed each of the novels selected, I noted in the margins whether the passage was a scene, a sequel, or something else. Many of the passages were clearly scenes or sequels, but quite a few included elements of both scenes and sequels. The novels I studied are examples of highly successful fiction, so I wasn't surprised to find few passages with unclear purpose. Chapters XXIX and XXX of *Moby-Dick* include elements of both scenes and sequels, but if Melville had deleted both, I wouldn't have missed them.[42]

Speaking from personal experience, I'd say that passages with elements of both scenes and sequels and no clear purpose most commonly appear in early drafts of a manuscript. One of my goals in self-editing—and I hope in yours, too—is to rewrite such passages or delete them.

PROBLEM-SOLVING PASSAGES

An example of a problem-solving passage can be found in *Hatchet*, where young Brian tries to figure out what he can eat in the wilderness.[43] The passage that begins with Brian's determination to find some food includes a clear goal (an element of scene) but no plan to achieve it (assessment of his situation, an element of a sequel). He digresses into recollection of a Thanksgiving meal at home, which only makes his saliva flow and his stomach growl (the emotion of frustration, which is an element of both scenes and sequels). He considers options (an element of the analysis phase of a sequel), such as finding lizards, but selects berries as his optimal choice. Brian plans a course of action that he hopes will let him find berries without getting lost before dark (planning is an element of the analysis phase of sequels). He makes a decision (which is the final phase of a sequel).

The passage described above could be classified as a sequel (with the elements of emotion, review, analysis, planning, and decision), or it could be classified as a scene (with a goal, multiple attempts, and a resolution).

Problem-solving passages are particularly useful in mystery stories. For example, Dan Brown uses problem-solving passages extensively in *The Da Vinci Code*.[44] They are also common in *The General's Daughter* by Nelson DeMille,[45] and in *Without Fail*, by Lee Child.[46]

In this chapter we have studied passages of writing that are *neither* scenes nor sequels, and we have examined passages that include elements of *both* scenes and sequels.

In the next chapter we will see how we can put our knowledge of scenes and sequels to use in troubleshooting a manuscript.

CHAPTER 9: TROUBLESHOOTING YOUR MANUSCRIPT, PART I

Has the following ever happened to you? After writing a passage of fiction, you know something is missing, but you can't quite put your finger on it. I suspect every writer has that experience sometimes. Apparently, even Ernest Hemingway struggled with this problem, as evidenced by his statement that "The first draft of anything is shit."

Whether or not you appreciate Hemingway's choice of words, the challenge remains of fixing an inadequate passage of writing—or even a whole manuscript. What can you do about a passage of fiction that doesn't work? You have a number of choices:

- Read and reread the passage, searching for the problem
- Hope for inspiration
- Put the writing away for a while and take a fresh look later
- Get someone else to critique the passage

- Apply a troubleshooting technique

Each of these alternatives has its advantages and disadvantages, but applying a troubleshooting technique has more benefits than the others. A troubleshooting technique relies on more than hope, may be performed immediately, and doesn't depend on other people to solve the problem.

There are probably as many different troubleshooting techniques as there are writers, but one stands out as consistently giving good results. In fact, I believe this technique may be the single most effective troubleshooting technique that a writer can apply to fiction.

This technique is also an absolute cure for writer's block. Whatever piece of fiction you find yourself stuck on, use this technique and you will be back to writing in no time. The power to prevent or unlock writer's block puts you, the author, in charge and not subject to the whims of inspiration.

The technique I'm referring to is *scene-and-sequel analysis*. As the name implies, scene-and-sequel analysis is a detailed study of the scenes and sequels in a manuscript. Just as a surgeon must have a thorough knowledge of human anatomy before slicing into someone, scene-and-sequel analysis requires a thorough understanding of the structure of scenes and sequels. Fortunately, after reading the first few chapters of this book, you now have that knowledge.

For the purposes of troubleshooting, whether or not you consciously wrote scenes and sequels when you drafted the manuscript is irrelevant. If your manuscript includes a character trying to accomplish a goal (and I hope it does), then you have at least one scene. If your manuscript includes at least one passage in which a character has a reflective response to success or failure (and I hope it does), then your writing includes at least one sequel. More than likely, your manuscript includes many scenes and sequels, even if you didn't have that concept in mind when you wrote them.

Let's put scene-and-sequel analysis in perspective before we move on. Scene-and-sequel analysis is meant to be a problem-solving tool, a technique for exploring a passage of writing in order to see passages that could be improved—not a straightjacket for turning writers into slaves of a technique or style. Most likely, your manuscript already includes scenes and sequels, but it probably also includes *fragments* of scenes and sequels, passages that resemble *neither* scenes nor sequels, and passages that include elements of *both* scenes and sequels. All of this is okay, if the writing works acceptably to advance the story. You as the writer decide how much your final product does or does not resemble fully developed scenes and sequels—or something else.

I've made a couple of assumptions regarding your writing, just as I do with my own.

1. You are troubleshooting only the passages of writing that you think need improvement.
2. Almost any passage of writing can be improved.

Flexibility is a key to writing scenes and sequels that create an emotional roller coaster with ups, downs, twists, and turns. To meet the needs of the story, scenes and sequels (and their various components) may be lengthened, shortened, skipped, or reorganized. As Bickham explained, scenes and sequels may be "devilishly difficult"[47] to recognize in published novels precisely because their authors tailored their use to fit the needs of the story.

Unless you have consciously constructed your manuscript with fully developed scenes and sequels, they may be a challenge to identify. I intentionally write scenes and sequels, but the casual reader of my stories probably wouldn't notice that. Confession: in my final draft, I sometimes have to look closely to identify where a scene ends and another scene or a sequel begins, but that's the way it should be.

As I mentioned earlier, your manuscript probably consists of a mixture of scenes, sequels, transitions, fragments of scenes and sequels, passages that don't resemble *either* scenes or sequels, and passages that resemble *both* scenes and sequels. That's okay if your manuscript works the way you want it to, but let's assume you need to improve your writing.

Let's do some troubleshooting. From your own manuscript, select a passage of writing at least several pages long that needs improvement. Alternatively, just select the passage of fiction you are currently writing.

SCENE, SEQUEL, OR SOMETHING ELSE

The first step in troubleshooting a passage of writing is to determine whether it is a scene, a sequel, or something else. What's the easiest way to recognize scenes and sequels? Let's review the definition of each word. A *scene* is a passage of writing in which a character attempts to achieve a goal. A *sequel* is a character's reflective reaction to the ending of a scene.

Using these bare-bones definitions, see if your character is trying to accomplish a goal. If so, then it's a scene. If your character is licking his wounds after defeat or patting himself on the back after a victory, then your passage is a sequel. If your character isn't trying to accomplish a goal *and* he isn't reflecting on failure or success, then the passage is neither a scene nor a sequel.

Scene-and-sequel analysis can be a lot like unraveling a tangled fishing line: you may have to coax each strand free before you achieve real progress. For example, the character's goal may not be *stated* in the scene. Here's a tip: if the character in a passage is trying to accomplish something, you may assume that the character's goal is to accomplish that something. Scene goals are frequently implied or assumed rather than stated.

Recognizing the beginning and ending of scenes and sequels can be challenging. Scenes and sequels may be interrupted by a sudden change in the story. For example, partway through a scene or sequel, a man holding a gun enters the room. The scene or sequel ends immediately, creating a fragment or a truncated scene or sequel, and a new scene begins, probably with the character adopting a new goal (such as to avoid being shot).

SCENE ANALYSIS

What if you determine that your passage is a scene? The next step is to compare it to the prototype scene in Chapter 2. You will find a Prototype-Scene Analysis worksheet below. Carefully dissect your scene to identify the various components of a prototype scene and record them on a *copy* of the worksheet. Note any prototype components missing from your scene, but also note any extra elements in your scene that do not correspond to the components of the prototype

TROUBLESHOOTING WORKSHEET
PROTOTYPE-SCENE ANALYSIS

Manuscript: Title_____ Chapter#_____Page# ____ Line #____

SETTING

- Place

- Time

- Character

- Point of View

- Character's Situation

- Crucible

CHARACTER'S GOAL

STAKES

MOTIVATION

ATTEMPT # 1

RESISTANCE #1

ATTEMPT # 2

RESISTANCE # 2

ATTEMPT # 3

RESISTANCE #3

RESOLUTION

Once you have completed this task, consider whether adding missing components to your scene would improve it. For example, does the character's goal involve enough stakes that matter to the character and the reader? Does the character attempt to achieve his goal three times? Does the scene need additional (or stronger) elements of resistance?

If your passage includes more parts than are named on the prototype worksheet, consider whether those parts should be deleted or how they could be transformed to fit the prototype. Study each part of your scene. How could it be improved? Should it be lengthened, shortened, or deleted? This is an appropriate time to brainstorm, to release your inner child, and to put yourself in the mind of your character and let your creative juices flow.

SEQUEL ANALYSIS

What if you determine that your passage is a sequel? Compare the passage from your manuscript to a copy of the Prototype-Sequel Analysis worksheet shown below. Note any missing parts and any extra parts. Will making your sequel more like the prototype improve it? Put yourself in the consciousness of your character and give your imagination free rein.

TROUBLESHOOTING WORKSHEET
PROTOTYPE-SEQUEL ANALYSIS

Manuscript: Title_____ Chapter#____ Page# ___ Line #___

SETTING

- Place

- Time

- Character

- Point of View

- Character's Situation

- Crucible

EMOTION

REVIEW

ANALYISIS

PLANNING

DECISION

ACTION TO IMPLEMENT DECISION (begins new scene)

NEITHER SCENE NOR SEQUEL

You may have written a passage that is *neither* a scene nor a sequel. How is that possible? If your passage doesn't have a character attempting to achieve a goal or a character reflecting on success or failure, then it is something else. That something else could be a passage of narration, description, a transition, a chunk of dialogue, or a character mentally wandering through whatever is on his mind.

Okay, so you have determined that your passage is neither a scene nor a sequel. What troubleshooting technique could you apply? If your passage is neither a scene nor a sequel, then nothing much happens in it. That probably explains why it doesn't work. You have several choices: (1) convert the passage to a scene, (2) convert the passage to a sequel, or (3) reevaluate the purpose of the passage and then decide whether or not to keep it.

To convert a passage to a scene, give the character a goal, have him attempt to achieve it, and frustrate his attempts with resistance. Then work toward making the scene more like the prototype scene. Alternatively, show the character reflecting on failure or success, then build a sequel, using the prototype as a guide. If the passage doesn't convert to either a scene or a sequel, ask yourself why it needs to be in your manuscript, then proceed from there.

ELEMENTS OF BOTH SCENES AND SEQUELS

Suppose the passage includes elements of *both* scenes and sequels. Carefully review your passage and consider its purpose. Would the passage be better if the character was trying to achieve a goal or reflecting upon success or failure? What would happen if the passage was restructured to be more like a scene or more like a sequel? Should the passage be split into a fully developed scene *and* a fully developed sequel?

Fragments are snippets of writing that could be part of a scene or a sequel or anything else. Fragments may be useful in a variety of circumstances, but consider what would happen if you expanded a fragment into a full scene or sequel or simply deleted it.

Although a *sequel* is defined as what comes after a scene, a sequel may be included without portraying the scene it follows. That's right: a sequel can show the character reacting to a scene that wasn't written. Why would you do this? To vary the pace or to explore the *why* of an event or its emotional aspect, as opposed to the event itself. Since sequels are by definition reflective, they make great vehicles for sharing information. At any point in a story where new information needs to be shared, consider structuring that passage as sequel.

Likewise, scenes may follow one another without having sequels between them. If a character can move from one scene to another without bridging them with a sequel, so be it. Fast-paced fiction, such as thrillers, frequently present one scene after another with few breaks between them.

A passage that includes elements of both scenes and sequels may be a problem-solving passage. If so, consider whether the passage would be more effective if structured more like a scene or more like a sequel. Also ask yourself if some additional elements of scenes and sequels could improve your problem-solving passage.

The purpose of scene-and-sequel analysis is to improve a passage of writing, not to impose a requirement that each passage of writing be structured like a prototype scene or sequel. If the analysis helped you improve the passage, it worked. Declare victory and move on.

Do yourself a favor and give scene-and-sequel analysis a try. You'll know it works when your writing becomes more effective.

In this chapter we have seen that using a troubleshooting technique may help you to improve a passage. We have learned how scene-and-sequel analysis works. We have looked at specific techniques for troubleshooting scenes, sequels, passages that are neither scenes nor sequels, and passages that include elements of both scenes and sequels.

In the next chapter we will use scene-and-sequel analysis to troubleshoot a specific story.

CHAPTER 10: TROUBLESHOOTING YOUR MANUSCRIPT, PART II

Let's do some troubleshooting. To keep this exercise manageable, I've selected a short piece of writing, *Goldilocks and the Three Bears*, as our example. There are variations of the story, but most resemble this one.

Once upon a time, there was a little girl named Goldilocks. She went for a walk in the forest. Soon she came to a house. She knocked, and when no one answered, she walked right in.

At the table in the kitchen, there were three bowls of porridge. Goldilocks was hungry. She tasted the porridge from the first bowl.

"This porridge is too hot!" she said.

She tasted the porridge from the second bowl.

"This porridge is too cold," she said.

So she tasted the last bowl of porridge.

"Ahhh, this porridge is just right," she said happily, and she ate it all up.

When she had finished eating, she decided she was feeling a little tired. So she walked into the living room, where she saw three chairs. Goldilocks sat in the first chair.

"This chair is too big!" she said.

So she sat in the second chair.

"This chair is too big, too!" she said.

So she tried the last and smallest chair.

"Ahhh, this chair is just right," she said. But just as she settled into the chair, it broke into pieces!

Goldilocks was very tired by this time, so she went upstairs to the bedroom. She lay down on the first bed, but it was too hard. Then she lay in the second bed, but it was too soft. She tried the third bed, and it was just right. Goldilocks fell asleep.

As she was sleeping, the three bears came home.

"Someone's been eating my porridge," growled the papa bear.

"Someone's been eating my porridge," said the mama bear.

"Someone's been eating my porridge, and they ate it all up!" said the baby bear.

"Someone's been sitting in my chair," said the papa bear.

"Someone's been sitting in my chair," said the mama bear.

"Someone's been sitting in my chair, and they broke it all to pieces," said the baby bear.

They decided to look around, and when they got upstairs to the bedroom, the papa bear growled. "Someone's been sleeping in my bed."

"Someone's been sleeping in my bed, too," said the mama bear.

"Someone's been sleeping in my bed, and she's still there!" cried the baby bear.

Just then, Goldilocks woke up and saw the three bears. She screamed "Help!" And she jumped up and ran out of the room. Goldilocks ran down the stairs, opened the door, and ran away into the forest. And she never returned to the home of the three bears.

TROUBLESHOOTING GOLDILOCKS

Years ago, when I was a young father, I read *Goldilocks and the Three Bears* to my kids. To me the story seemed to lack something, but I wasn't sure what. Let's use scene-and-sequel analysis and see if we can improve on the traditional telling of the tale.

First, let's address the overall story. The basic premise is that a girl enters someone else's home without permission, steals their food, breaks their furniture, then violates the privacy of their bedroom. Although Goldilocks behaves badly, she gets away scot-free. This summary raises questions about Goldilocks's character and the theme of the story, so let's keep them in mind as we continue our analysis.

Now let's identify the scenes and sequels in the story and their components (in parentheses).

> Once upon a time, there was a little girl named Goldilocks. She went for a walk in the forest. Soon, she came to a house. (SCENE SETUP)
>
> She knocked, and when no one answered, she walked right in. (FIRST AND SECOND ATTEMPTS)

At the table in the kitchen, there were three bowls of porridge. Goldilocks was hungry. (SCENE SETUP)

She tasted the porridge from the first bowl. (FIRST ATTEMPT)

"This porridge is too hot!" she said. (ATTEMPT FAILS)

She tasted the porridge from the second bowl. (SECOND ATTEMPT)

"This porridge is too cold," she said. (ATTEMPT FAILS)

So she tasted the last bowl of porridge. (THIRD ATTEMPT)

"Ahhh, this porridge is just right," she said happily, and she ate it all up. (ATTEMPT IS SUCCESSFUL)

When she had finished eating, she decided she was feeling a little tired. (SEQUEL)

So she walked into the living room, where she saw three chairs. (SCENE SETUP)

Goldilocks sat in the first chair. (FIRST ATTEMPT)

"This chair is too big!" she said. (ATTEMPT FAILS)

So she sat in the second chair. (SECOND ATTEMPT)

"This chair is too big, too!" she said. (ATTEMPT FAILS)

So she tried the last and smallest chair. (THIRD ATTEMPT)

"Ahhh, this chair is just right," she said. But just as she settled into the chair, it broke into pieces! (ATTEMPT FAILS)

Goldilocks was very tired by this time, so she went upstairs to the bedroom. (SCENE SETUP)

She lay down on the first bed, but it was too hard. (FIRST ATTEMPT FAILS)

Then she lay in the second bed, but it was too soft. (SECOND ATTEMPT FAILS)

She tried the third bed, and it was just right. Goldilocks fell asleep. (THIRD ATTEMPT SUCCEEDS)

As she was sleeping, the three bears came home. (SCENE SETUP)

"Someone's been eating my porridge," growled the papa bear. (FIRST ATTEMPT)

"Someone's been eating my porridge," said the mama bear. (SECOND ATTEMPT)

"Someone's been eating my porridge, and they ate it all up!" said the baby bear. (THIRD ATTEMPT)

"Someone's been sitting in my chair," said the papa bear. (FIRST ATTEMPT)

"Someone's been sitting in my chair," said the mama bear. (SECOND ATTEMPT)

"Someone's been sitting in my chair, and they broke it all to pieces," said the baby bear. (THIRD ATTEMPT)

They decided to look around, and when they got upstairs to the bedroom, the papa bear growled. (SCENE SETUP)

"Someone's been sleeping in my bed." (FIRST ATTEMPT)

"Someone's been sleeping in my bed, too," said the mama bear. (SECOND ATTEMPT)

"Someone's been sleeping in my bed, and she's still there!" cried the baby bear. (THIRD ATTEMPT IS SUCCESSFUL)

Just then, Goldilocks woke up and saw the three bears. (SCENE SETUP)

She screamed "Help!" (FIRST ATTEMPT)

And she jumped up and ran out of the room. (SECOND ATTEMPT)

Goldilocks ran down the stairs, opened the door, and ran away into the forest. (THIRD ATTEMPT)

And she never returned to the home of the three bears. (RESOLUTION)

Let's compare the parts of the traditional telling of *The Story of Goldilocks and the Three Bears* to the prototype scene-and-sequel analysis worksheets provided in the previous chapter.

Starting with the story's initial setup, I noticed that it establishes place (forest), time (once upon a time), focal character (Goldilocks), point of view (omniscient third-person), but it doesn't identify the character's situation, the crucible, the character's goal, or any stakes. My version expands the setup as follows.

Once upon a time, in a land far, far away, a girl named Goldilocks went for a long walk in the forest. She forgot to bring food with her, and after a while her stomach ached with hunger. She came upon a

house in the woods and decided to ask for something
to eat.

This version of the setup describes the character's overall situation, creates a crucible (a long walk implies that she is far from home), declares her goal to find something to eat, and implies that if she doesn't find something to eat, she will go hungry (stakes).

The traditional telling of the story continues with the first scene as follows:

She knocked, and when no one answered, she
walked right in. (FIRST AND SECOND ATTEMPTS)

This scene seems a little skimpy, so let's expand it by making it more like a prototype scene.

Goldilocks knew that the forest could be a dangerous place, and she didn't know who lived in the house. She didn't see anyone, so she crept close and peeked in the window. Not seeing anything scary, she knocked on the door. When no one answered, Goldilocks opened the door and yelled, "Is anyone home!" She waited a moment, ready to run away if she heard or saw anything scary.

This version expands the first scene to include three attempts (1) looking around for danger, (2) peeking inside, and (3) opening the door and yelling. Each of these attempts results in partial failure (no one willing to feed her) and partial success (nothing scary appeared, either).

The traditional version does not include a sequel, so let's add one.

Goldilocks could feel her heart beating fast. She was standing in the doorway of a house where someone or something might not act friendly toward her. If she left now, she would be very hungry, but she would get home eventually. She knew that going into someone else's home without being invited was wrong. She decided that a little hunger was better than being attacked by something scary, so she decided to head home.

This sequel includes emotion (fear, as evidenced by her rapid heartbeat). Goldilocks reviews her situation (standing in the doorway, hoping for food). She considers her options (going home or entering someone else's house). Her decision to head home marks an end to the sequel, and we are ready for the next scene.

> Just as Goldilocks started to close the door and leave, she smelled something delicious. Her stomach growled with hunger, and she decided to see what smelled so good. She stepped into the house, and the smell drew her to the kitchen. On a table were three bowls of porridge.

This is a short scene, with only one attempt (looking for food), which results in success. The traditional story doesn't include a sequel here, so let's add one.

> Goldilocks giggled with delight. Porridge was one of her favorite foods. Then she frowned. She had entered someone else's house without permission. She also knew that taking someone else's food was wrong. The owners of the house might return at any moment, and they might be really angry with her. Whatever she was going to do, she had better do it quickly. She should leave right now, she thought, and run all the

way home. But the porridge smelled so good, and her stomach ached with hunger. Goldilocks looked out the window to make sure no one was coming home. Seeing nothing, she decided to try just a teen-sy-weensy taste.

This sequel resembles the prototype by starting with emotion (delight), moving to review of past events (entering the house), analyzing the situation (home invasion, stealing food, danger of the homeowners' return), planning (do something quickly, run for home, and check for approaching homeowners), and making a decision (trying just a taste). Now we are ready for the next scene, which is pretty close to the traditional telling.

Goldilocks picked up a spoon and tasted the porridge in the first bowl. "Ouch!" she said. "This porridge is too hot."

She tasted the porridge from the second bowl. "Oooh!" she said. "This porridge is too cold."

She tasted the last bowl of porridge. "Ahhh!" she said. "This porridge is just right." And she ate it all up.

This scene closely resembles the prototype in that it includes three attempts, the first two of which end in disappointment. The traditional telling includes a one-sentence sequel.

After she'd eaten the breakfast, she decided she was feeling a little tired.

Let's expand that sequel to look more like the prototype.

Goldilocks sighed as she set the spoon on the table. She felt better now that her stomach was full, but she felt guilty for eating someone else's breakfast. Somebody's going to be unhappy with me, she figured.

Goldilocks knew she should leave the house and go home, but then she noticed three chairs in the next room. They looked so comfortable, and she was so tired. Goldilocks peeked out the window to make sure no one was coming home, then decided she had time for a little rest.

Now let's move to the next scene, largely with the traditional telling, which closely resembles the prototype.

Goldilocks climbed into the first chair. After a moment, she said, "This chair is too big!"

So she climbed down and hopped into the second chair. "This chair is too big, too!" she said.

So she hopped down and tried the last and smallest chair. "Ahhh!" she said. "This chair is just right." But just then the chair broke into pieces, and Goldilocks tumbled to the floor.

Let's add a sequel here.

Goldilocks felt bad that she had broken someone's chair, especially after eating their breakfast. She peeked out the window to make sure no one was coming. I should leave right now, she thought, but I'm so, so tired. She noticed a stairway and figured there must be a bedroom upstairs. She decided to take a little nap.

The next scene is largely the traditional telling.

Goldilocks ran up the stairs, and sure enough, she found a room with three beds.

She lay down on the first bed. "Ouch!" she said. "This one is too hard."

She tried the second bed, but it was too soft.

She lay down in the third bed, and it was just right. Goldilocks soon fell fast asleep.

The story now shifts from the focal character of Goldilocks to that of the three bears. The traditional setup for the bears is a little skimpy, so let's expand it before moving on to the next scene.

Three bears had been walking in the forest while their breakfast cooled. When they returned home, they found their front door wide open, and they growled.

The next scene is largely the traditional telling.

They walked into their kitchen, and the papa bear growled. "Someone's been eating my porridge."

The mama bear growled. "Someone's been eating my porridge."

The baby bear cried. "Someone's been eating my porridge, and they ate it all up!"

Let's insert a short sequel.

The three bears were very unhappy that some-one had eaten their breakfast. They wondered if that someone had been up to more mischief in their house. They decided to look around.

The next scene is largely the traditional telling.

They went into the next room, and the papa bear growled. "Someone's been sitting in my chair."

The mama bear growled. "Someone's been sit-ting in my chair."

The baby bear cried. "Someone's been sitting in my chair, and they broke it all to pieces!"

Let's add a sequel fragment (a decision).

The three bears decided to look around some more.

And now back to the traditionally told scene.

When they got upstairs, the papa bear growled. "Someone's been sleeping in my bed."

The mama bear growled. "Someone's been sleeping in my bed, too."

The baby bear growled. "Someone's been sleeping in my bed, and she's still there!"

The classic telling of this story lets Goldilocks off the hook for her transgressions. Let's modify the ending in a manner consistent with many other folk tales (think of a wolf eating a boy, a pig boiling a wolf alive, and a little boy and girl pushing a witch into a hot oven).

Just then, Goldilocks woke up and saw the three bears. She screamed and jumped out of bed, ready to run away.

The three bears roared. They caught Goldilocks, ripped her to pieces, and gobbled her all up.

And no one ever saw Goldilocks again.

Notice how the use of scene-and-sequel analysis opens the story, much like a flower blooming. Keep in mind that scene-and-sequel analysis does not necessarily result in a finished product.

The analysis produces a new first draft, which you will need to further revise.

I have enjoyed retelling *The Story of Goldilocks and the Three Bears*, and I hope you did, too. Whether or not you like the retold version better than the classic story, I trust that this exercise has effectively demonstrated to you the power of scene-and-sequel analysis as a means of reworking a passage of writing.

In the next chapter we will look at how to use scenes and sequels to pace the story, arrange the pieces, and structure the chapters.

CHAPTER 11: PUTTING IT ALL TOGETHER

CHAPTER CONTENTS

- Pacing with scenes and sequels
- Arranging the pieces
- Chapters vs. scenes and sequels
- Chapter endings
- Chapter beginnings
- Sections

PACING WITH SCENES AND SEQUELS

Scenes and sequels, by their nature, have a different pace. Scenes propel the story forward as the focal character attempts to achieve an objective. Scenes tend to be exciting, action-packed, fast reading. Sequels provide a breather while the character sorts out his feelings, reviews events, analyzes his situation, plans his next move, and makes a decision. Sequels tend to be emotional, thought-packed, slower reading.

The tempo difference between scenes and sequels creates an opportunity to use them in combination to set the rhythm and pace of the entire story. If you wish to accelerate the pace of your story, build up your scenes and condense (or hide) the sequels. If you wish to slow the pace of your story, do just the opposite: build up the sequels and trim the scenes.

Each of the novels I analyzed was largely constructed of scenes and sequels, even though the method of their use and the pace of each one varied considerably. The information in this book provides you with everything you need to create effective scenes and sequels. The pacing power of using scenes and sequels in combination gives you another tool to create a novel that readers have difficulty setting aside.

ARRANGING THE PIECES

The novels I analyzed ranged from seemingly simple construction to those that appeared to be substantially more complicated, yet each one consisted of the following parts:

- Scenes
- Sequels
- Fragments of scenes
- Fragments of sequels

- Passages that are neither scenes nor sequels
- Passages that include elements of both scenes and sequels

When I began my analysis, I expected that stories would logically begin with a scene, then flow to a sequel and then back to a scene, over and over again. What I found was quite different.

I initially assumed that the first chapter of a story would begin with a scene then flow to a sequel. Some novels have that structure,[48] but some novels begin with a sequel.[4950]

I assumed that a sequel would follow each scene, as night follows day in real life. In reality, a novel may include a series of scenes, one right after another, with minimal transition between them.

I was surprised to see a multitude of *fragments* of both scenes and sequels. I also found an abundance of passages that were *neither* scenes nor sequels—or just the opposite, with passage that included components of *both* scenes and sequels.

Quite a few of the novels included multiple scenes early in the story as the character is charging ahead or responding to multiple events.[515253] Often the frequency of sequels increased as the story progressed. I assumed that if an author used a prologue, that prologue would be structured as a scene, but Stephenie Meyer used a prologue to set up *Twilight*, and it is structured as a fragment of a sequel.

One of the discoveries I hoped to make was how scenes and sequels are used differently when the story is presented in first person rather than third person. I found no difference in the presentation of scenes and sequels, whether the story was written in first person or third.

When I first analyzed *The Da Vinci Code*, by Dan Brown, I promptly labeled it as the most complicated in structure of the books I had studied. Later in my analysis, I realized that Brown's use of scenes and sequels is consistent with that of the other authors. What makes *The Da Vinci Code* appear more complicated is the extensive cast of characters from whose perspective Brown tells the story, often with multiple points of view within the same chapter.

Scenes and sequels written in a multitude of variations comprise the bulk of the novels I studied. The arrangement of those scenes and sequels, together with fragments, passages that were neither scenes nor sequels, and passages that included components of both scenes and sequels varied considerably from one story to the next.

CHAPTER VS. SCENES AND SEQUELS

Previously, I defined a *chapter* as a segment of writing delineated by chapter breaks. You probably noticed that this definition doesn't mention scenes and sequels. That's because the main purpose of a chapter is to show the reader that the novel has points at which the reader can logically put the book down, to be continued another time—to show the reader that the novel isn't one big, intimidating monolith of text.

Of course, the goal of providing readers with logical break points where they can pause is at cross purposes with your goal to create a page-turner—fiction that the reader can't put down, cover to cover.

This is not to say that scenes and sequels have nothing to do with chapters. That couldn't be further from the truth. In fact, strategic chapter placement is highly dependent upon scenes and sequels. First let's look at the possibilities.

A classic method of presenting chapters is to show both a scene and the subsequent sequel in the same chapter: the chapter starts at the beginning of the scene and ends at the conclusion of the sequel. Such an arrangement is logical, and it creates a tidy package for a chapter.

CHAPTER BREAK

- SCENE

- SEQUEL

CHAPTER BREAK

A similar strategy is for a chapter to include a single scene only.

CHAPTER BREAK

- SCENE

CHAPTER BREAK

Then the next chapter could include the subsequent sequel.

CHAPTER BREAK

- SEQUEL

CHAPTER BREAK

An example of the effective use of this structure can be seen in *The Lucky One* by Nicholas Sparks, where chapters 14 and 17 feature the antagonist Keith Clayton licking his wounds, patting himself on the back, or planning additional mischief.[54]

A chapter may include many scenes.

CHAPTER BREAK

- SCENE

- SCENE

- SCENE

CHAPTER BREAK

Examples of two or more scenes per chapter abound in thriller novels, where sequels are often not portrayed.

If you can have multiple scenes in one chapter, why not multiple sequels?

CHAPTER BREAK

- SEQUEL

- SEQUEL

- SEQUEL

CHAPTER BREAK

In *Jurassic Park*, Michael Crichton uses this structure in the chapter titled "Welcome," where three viewpoint characters each have a separate sequel.[55]

An example of this structure might also occur in a romance novel, where star-crossed lovers each react reflectively to a previous scene. In a love triangle, a third sequel could be included.

So far we have assumed that an entire scene or sequel is included in a chapter, but that isn't necessarily how novels are structured. Let's look at the prototype scene and sequel in the context of a chapter.

CHAPTER BREAK

- SCENE
    - SCENE SETUP
    - ATTEMPT #1
    - ATTEMPT #2
    - ATTEMPT #3
    - RESOLUTION
- SEQUEL
    - EMOTION
    - REVIEW
    - ANALYSIS
    - PLANNING
    - DECISION

CHAPTER BREAK

A chapter could include an incomplete scene that the writer then finishes in a later chapter.

CHAPTER BREAK

- SCENE
    - SCENE SETUP
    - ATTEMPT #1
    - ATTEMPT #2
    - ATTEMPT #3

CHAPTER BREAK

    - CLIMAX
    - RESOLUTION

CHAPTER BREAK

This is a particularly agonizing structure for the reader, because the chapter ends just prior to the climax, leaving the reader panting in anticipation. This is the equivalent of a television show interrupted by a commercial just as the tension nears the breaking point.

In the previous example, the chapter ended near the end of a scene. You can also end a chapter near the beginning of a scene. Consider a chapter in which a hiker stumbles off a trail and finds himself clutching a rocky ledge atop a precipice. Such an event would certainly create a new short-term goal for the character (avoiding a fall), which would mark the beginning of a new scene.

CHAPTER BREAK

- SCENE

    o SCENE SETUP

    o ATTEMPT #1

CHAPTER BREAK

When placed at the end of a chapter, such a scene fragment is referred to as a *cliffhanger*.

Fragments may include any combination of scene or sequel parts arranged in any order needed to fit the story. A chapter may include a mixture of scenes, sequels, and fragments of scenes or sequels.

CHAPTER BREAK

- SEQUEL FRAGMENT

- SCENE

- SEQUEL FRAGMENT

- SCENE FRAGMENT

- SEQUEL

CHAPTER BREAK

Examples of this are abundant in *The Da Vinci Code* by Dan Brown. Chapters with this structure are easy to identify, because they include numerous section breaks.

CHAPTER ENDINGS

Chapter endings offer important page-turning opportunities. How you end a chapter largely determines whether the reader closes the book at that point. Once the reader closes the book, you always run the risk that he will never open it again. Our objective, then, is to end chapters in a manner that compels the reader to flip the page and continue reading. At the same time, we want to leave him with something that draws him back into our story at his next reading session.

ENDING WITH A SCENE

A logical place to end a chapter is at the end of a scene, particularly if the scene ends with some sort of setback for the character. What better time to end a scene than right after the character has failed to achieve his goal? An example of this is the first chapter of Stephenie Meyer's *Twilight*, where the chapter ending coincides with the scene depicting the conclusion of Bella's awful first day at a new school.[56]

You may, of course, end your chapter at any point in a scene, but some places are particularly effective. We have already seen that ending a chapter at the beginning of a new scene can be compelling. For example, in the second chapter of Gary Paulsen's *Hatchet*, young Brian finds himself in a small plane with a dead pilot. After a sequel in which he decides he must land the plane himself, Brian begins a new scene with action to execute his new plan: he points the nose of the plane down.[57] Then the chapter ends. How's that for a nail-biter?

Another place to end a chapter is in the middle of the action, such as right after the character's first attempt to achieve his goal. For example, in Sir Lancelot's attempt to rescue a damsel in distress, he quickly dispatches an enemy knight, only to see three more enemies rushing to fight him. A chapter ending at this point practically guarantees the reader will turn the page to find out what happens next.

ENDING WITH A SEQUEL

Sequels also provide opportunities to end a chapter, and a logical place to close a chapter is at the end of a sequel. After appropriate emotion and thinking, the character makes his decision, and the chapter ends. John Grisham uses this technique in *The Client* at the end of chapter 6 when the character decides that he will call an attorney.[58]

Why not end a chapter during or after the emotion phase of a sequel? For example, the character has just discovered that his longtime lover has betrayed him. The scene could end right there, of course, but the story might be better served if you show the character's emotional response, perhaps dropping to his knees and gasping for air.

How about closing a chapter during the review phase of a sequel? Stephenie Meyer ends chapter 9 of *Twilight* after Bella reviews what she knows about Edward: (1) he's a vampire, (2) he thirsts for her blood, and (3) she's in love with him.[59] I don't know about you, but after that chapter ending, I simply had to keep reading.

The analysis phase of a prototype sequel includes an evaluation of the situation. Let's say your character is a boxer who has just gotten knocked on his butt. You could end the chapter after a sequel fragment in which he realizes that winning this high-stakes fight is going to be a lot tougher than he thought.

Evaluating alternate courses of action can also be part of the thinking phase of a sequel. Imagine a sequel in which your character considers his options: (1) if he persists in the pursuit of his goal, he is likely to die a gruesome death, (2) if he fails to achieve his goal, the world will certainly be overtaken by an evil power. How's that for ending the chapter with your hero caught on the horns of a high-stakes dilemma? An alternative chapter ending during this phase of a sequel would come right after the character experiences an epiphany that reveals a new course of action.

The planning phase of a sequel offers another opportunity to close a chapter. In Chapter 7 of *Ender's Game*, a cadet slugs the main character. The chapter ends with Ender planning an alternative to revenge.[60]

ENDING WITH PROBLEM-SOLVING PASSAGES

Since problem-solving passages include components of both scenes and sequels, you can end a chapter using any of the techniques described above. *The General's Daughter* by Nelson DeMille contains numerous problem-solving passages, many of which DeMille ends with the main character stating a new goal after an implied or hidden sequel in which the character determines his next course of action. For example, chapter 4 ends when Brenner says, "Well, let's begin with the kitchen."[61] DeMille ends chapter 9 with "Rifle range 6, please."[62]

The Da Vinci Code by Dan Brown ends some problem-solving passages with a revelation—new information that stops the problem-solving effort in its tracks—in effect creating resistance to the character's effort to solve the problem. Such revelations can complicate the character's efforts, raise the stakes, or shrink the crucible by reducing the time or space in which the character has to operate. For example, in the first chapter of *The Da Vinci Code*, Robert Langdon is trying to make sense of a gruesome photograph. Dan Brown ends the chapter by having a policeman tell Landon, "You don't understand, Mr. Langdon. What you see in this photograph . . ." He paused. "Monsieur Sauniere did to himself."

CHAPTER BEGINNINGS

Scenes and sequels may also be used to design effective chapter beginnings. The objective of a page-turning chapter *ending* is to encourage the reader to continue to the next chapter. The objective of a page-turning chapter *beginning* is to entice the reader enough so that he is hooked by the story, after which you can reel him in at least until the end of the chapter. This will compel him to continue to the next chapter and to the next and the next until the end of the story.

Earlier we saw that chapters can *end* almost anywhere in either a scene or a sequel. Likewise, chapters can *begin* almost anywhere in either a scene or a sequel. Many chapters open at the beginning of a scene, and many open at the beginning of a sequel, but the novels I analyzed had plenty of examples of chapters that began *within* scenes or sequels. For example, in *The Lucky One*, Nicholas Sparks opens chapter 6 in the review phase of a sequel as the main character recalls his second tour in Iraq.[63] In *Hatchet*, Gary Paulsen opens chapter 8 with an obstacle that thwarts the character's attempt to reach his goal of getting a peaceful night's sleep when Brian awakes to the sound of an animal growling.[64] In *One for the Money*, Janet Evanovich opens chapter five with the decision phase of an otherwise hidden sequel: "I'd called Ranger and asked for help, since I was too chicken to do breaking and entering."[65]

SECTIONS

I've defined a *chapter* as a passage of writing delineated by chapter breaks, and I've defined a *section* as a passage of writing delineated by one or more section breaks. As with the definition of chapters, the definition of a section doesn't mention scenes or sequels. A *section break* is a form of punctuation that signals a change of viewpoint character or a significant change of time or location *within* a chapter.

Novels told from the viewpoint of a single character may use section breaks to signal a significant change of time[66] or place[67] within a chapter. Novels told from the viewpoint of two or more characters may also use section breaks to signal a change of viewpoint character within a chapter, as Dan Brown does frequently in *The Da Vinci Code* and John Grisham does in *The Client*.

This isn't to say that scenes and sequels have nothing to do with sections. Strategic section placement is highly dependent upon scenes and sequels, and much of the discussion above about chapters applies to section breaks. A chapter in a novel told from the perspective of many viewpoint characters may look like this.

CHAPTER BREAK

- SEQUEL FRAGMENT

SECTION BREAK

- SCENE

SECTION BREAK

- SEQUEL FRAGMENT

SECTION BREAK

- SCENE FRAGMENT

SECTION BREAK

- SEQUEL

CHAPTER BREAK

In this chapter we've seen how scenes and sequels can be arranged to pace your story, organize your story, and divide your story into chapters. We have also looked at how scenes and sequels can be used to end and start chapters. In addition, we examined how scenes and sequels relate to sections within a chapter.

In this book we've defined scenes and sequels, and we've studied the components of both scenes and sequels. We've reviewed formulas and developed a prototype for scenes and sequels. We've analyzed the benefits and the disadvantages of scenes and sequels. We've looked at variations in presentation and studied examples of scenes and sequels. We've studied passages of writing that are neither scenes nor sequels and looked at passages that include elements of both scenes and sequels. We've learned how to troubleshoot a passage using scene-and-sequel analysis. We've seen how to put all the pieces together to create page-turning fiction.

Happy fiction writing!

A PRACTICAL GLOSSARY OF FICTION-WRITING TERMS

Action. The fiction-writing mode of showing things happening, in detail, as they occur.

Active voice. Sentences structured so the subject performs the action of the verb. For example, *John* (subject) *danced* (verb).

Attribution. Words added to dialogue to tell the reader which character is speaking. For example, *He said, ". . ."*

Authorial intrusion. Obtrusive style, by which the author reveals himself to the reader.

Background. Information about the character that is relevant to the reader's understanding of the character's behavior and motivation.

Chapter. A passage or segment of writing delineated by chapter breaks.

Character. The *who* of a story. A character may be a person, an animal, or some other persona. A *focal character* is the person or entity attempting to achieve a goal within a scene.

Circumlocution. The use of many words to say something that could be said more clearly and directly by using few words. For example, instead of saying *guardians of the law*, saying *police*.

Cliché. Phrases, comparisons, expressions, or figures of speech that have been used so frequently they have lost their effectiveness.

Climax. That portion of a scene or story in which conflict and suspense peak prior to the resolution.

Conflict. A physical, verbal, or mental struggle between opposing forces.

Conversation (dialogue). The fiction-writing mode of presenting characters talking. Synonym: *dialogue*. Conversation is often accompanied by a verb of attribution, such as *said*. Dialogue may be categorized in four types: on-the nose, parallel, oblique, and subtext.

On-the-nose dialogue is conversation in which the speaker says exactly what he means, with no attempt to demur, deceive, be witty, use subterfuge, etc.

Parallel dialogue is conversation in which each segment of one character's dialogue responds to the previous segment of another's dialogue (one character asks a question or makes a statement, and the other character answers the question or follows up with a statement.).

Oblique dialogue is conversation in which a character does not respond logically to what another character just said. For example, (1) talking at cross-purposes, (2) answering unasked questions, (3) providing answers that sound like answers but really aren't, (4) changing subjects without warning, or (5) carrying on more than one conversation at a time.

Subtext dialogue is conversation in which the words spoken differ from what the speaker means. For example, if the speaker is hinting at something, attempting to deceive, or issuing a veiled threat.

Crucible. A plot situation which limits a character's choices of action.

Description. The fiction-writing mode for portraying people, places, things, or concepts. *Purple prose* is a type of description so elaborate, colorful, or flowery that it draws attention to itself.

Transmorphic description is a figure of speech that attributes human, god, animal, objects, concepts, or natural phenomenon with attributes of one another. For example, describing a human as a pit-bull terrier. Transmorphic description may be described using other, somewhat overlapping, terms such as *anthropomorphism, personification, objectification, prosopopoeia,* and *zoomorphism.*

Elements of fiction. The five major components of fiction: plot, character, setting, theme, and style.

Emotion. The fiction-writing mode of relating how a character feels.

Emotional complexity. Differing or conflicting emotions occurring simultaneously.

Epiphany. A character's sudden realization or burst of insight.

Euphemism. The substitution of a less offensive or more agreeable term for another one. For example, "Billy stepped behind the bushes *to answer the call of nature.*"

Expletive. A "filler" word that contributes little if anything to the meaning of the sentence. Expletives may be classified into three categories: syntactic expletives, expletive attributives, and bad language. A *syntactic expletive* is a filler word that does not contribute meaning to the sentence. Examples include *it* and *there* when used as a dummy subject, as in *It is hot today* or *There will come a time for revenge.* An *expletive attributive* is a modifier that contributes little, if anything, to the meaning of the sentence. An expletive attributive may suggest strength of feeling (anger, irritation, admiration) and thus become a grammatical intensifier. For example, *damn, bloody,* and *wretched,* as in:

They disconnected the *damned* phone.

The politicians had better get their *bloody* act together.

He had to obey the *wretched* order.

Bad language is vulgar, obscene, or profane language.

Exposition. The fiction-writing mode of conveying information.

Expository device. Various devices used by an author to convey information in fiction. Classic examples include props such as treasure maps and messages in bottles. Others include newspaper clippings, letters, diaries, and trial transcriptions. The advancement of technology has provided new expository devices: e-mails, text messages, podcasts. In the world of science fiction and fantasy, expository devices are limited only by the writer's imagination.

External plot. The overarching plotline of a story.

Fiction-writing mode. One of eleven types of writing used by authors to construct stories. See *description, action, narration, conversation, exposition, summarization, introspection, sensation, transition, emotion, recollection.*

Figure of speech. A technique of using words in other than their usual manner to suggest an image, emotion, sensation, tone, or other effect. For example, circumlocution, euphemism, extended metaphor, hyperbole, idiom, innuendo, irony, metaphor, mixed metaphor, simile.

Flashback. A scene that interrupts the real-time of the story while the character relives a past event.

Flashforward. A scene that interrupts the real-time of the story while the character "experiences" a future event.

Flow of dialogue. The rhythm and pace of dialogue.

Forecasting. Words by which the author or narrator alerts the reader to what may lie ahead in the story. For example, *Little did Robin know that he would soon be . . .*

Foreshadowing. Words which subtly prepare the reader for an upcoming event. For example, prior to an earthquake, having a character view fallen stalactites in a cave, then wonder if a quake had knocked them down.

Goal. Something desired by the character. A character may have a primary goal for the duration of the story. The character may have a shorter-term goal in each scene.

Hyperbole. An exaggeration of a statement. For example, "The harpoon weighed a *ton.*"

Idiom. An expression whose meaning is not predictable from the usual meanings of its constituent elements. For example, *After a two-year engagement, they* tied the knot *in front of family and friends.*

Imagery. Writing in a manner that stimulates an illusion of sensory perception.

Immediacy. The degree to which a story unfolds as it is being told, helping the reader maintain the illusion that he's *experiencing* the events of the story rather than reading or hearing them after the fact. Immediacy ranges from delayed to immediate.

Incidental action. Small amounts of activity, such as gestures, mannerisms, and body language.

Information dump. An excess of information presented at one time.

Innuendo. A hidden meaning in a sentence that makes sense whether or not the hidden meaning is detected by the reader or listener. For example, *At the end of their first date, Arty told Jenny he* would like to see more of her. Taken literally, Arty would like to see Jenny again. The phrase could also mean that Arty would like to see more of Jenny's body.

Internal plot. A character's emotional, mental, or spiritual journey, coincident with the story's overarching plot.

Introspection. The fiction-writing mode of sharing a character's thinking. Introspection is often facilitated by the use of a *verb of thought,* such as *think, hope, wonder, pray, reason, realize, decide.* Introspection may be categorized in two types: direct and indirect. *Direct introspection* shares a character's thoughts, written in that character's exact words in first person, present tense. For example, *I hope Bill will listen to reason before someone gets hurt.* *Indirect introspection* reveals a character's thoughts written in summary or paraphrased form. For example, *Charles hoped Bill would listen to reason.*

Irony. A figure of speech in which words are used in a manner to convey a meaning opposite to their usual meaning. For example, *Al saw that the thermometer had risen to three degrees Fahrenheit,* a real heat wave.

Melodramatic. Inappropriate, excessive, exaggerated, or indulgent effort to sensationalize fiction.

Metaphor. Explicitly stating that one entity *is* another for the purpose of suggesting a resemblance. For example, *Number 64, the left tackle, is a tank.* A *mixed metaphor* is a figure of speech that combines elements of unrelated metaphors, resulting in incongruous comparisons. For example, *He's barking up the wrong tree* is a metaphor and so is *He's up the creek without a paddle.* But *He's barking up the wrong creek* is a mixed metaphor.

An *extended metaphor* is a metaphor continued into subsequent sentences or even throughout a story. William Shakespeare wrote one of the most well known extended metaphors:

"All the world's a stage. And all men and women merely players. They have their exits and their entrances. And one man in his time plays many parts . . ." (*As You Like It*, Act II, Scene VII).

Milieu. The setting of a story, including its social, geographical, and political context. Synonym: setting.

Modifier. Words, such as adjectives and adverbs, that change the meaning of another word. An *intensifier* is a modifier that amplifies the meaning of the word it modifies. For example, *The* extremely *miffed giant climbed down the beanstalk.* A *qualifier* is a modifier that weakens the word modified. For example, *The* slightly *miffed giant climbed down the beanstalk.*

Motivation. A need, idea, or emotion that compels a character to take action.

Narration. The fiction-writing mode by which the narrator communicates directly to the reader. Narration may be divided into two types: unobtrusive and obtrusive.

Unobtrusive narration is communication from the narrator that is so subtle that there appears to be no narrator.

Obtrusive narration is communication that draws attention to the narrator. Obtrusive narration may be categorized into three types: direct-address narration, reminder narration, and foreshadowing narration.

Direct-address narration names the reader. For example, *Now, dear reader, little does Bartholomew know . . .*

Reminder narration is a statement made by the narrator to help the reader recall what has previously transpired in the story. For example, *As you recall, at the beginning of the story . . .*

Forecasting narration is communication by which the narrator alerts the reader to what may lie ahead in the story. For example, *Little did Robin know that he would soon be . . .*

Narrative distance. The sense of proximity between the narrator of written fiction and the subject matter of the story, including characters, events, and setting. Ranges from distant to close to intimate.

Obstacle. Something that blocks, delays, or complicates a character's attempt to achieve his goal.

Obtrusiveness. Writing that draws attention to itself and thus to the author and/or narrator of the story.

Parallelism. The use of similar structures in adjacent words or phrases. Parallelism may be used in short sentences, sentences presenting a series of items, or in longer, more complicated expressions. For example,

Easy come, easy go.

She likes hunting, fishing, and riding.

"The inherent vice of capitalism is the unequal sharing of a blessing; the inherent virtue of socialism is the equal sharing of miseries."—Winston Churchill

Passage of writing. Two or more paragraphs with some common purpose. Synonym: segment of writing.

Passive voice. Sentences structured so the subject of the sentence does not perform the action of the verb. For example, *The ball* (subject) *was hit* (verb).

Plot. The "what happens" in a story. A series of events presented in a manner designed to create dramatic effect.

Point of view. The character or persona through whom a story is told.

Punctuation. A set of symbols used by the author to guide the reader as to how the writing should be read.

Real time of the story. The "now" of a story as it unfolds.

Recollection. The fiction-writing mode for revealing what a character remembers. Recollection may be accompanied by a verb of recollection or a verb phrase used to facilitate a character's recollection. For example, *remembered, recalled, called to mind, thought back to, reminisced.*

Resolution. How a scene or story ends after the climax.

Response. A reaction to stimulus.

Rhythm. The cadence of words in a passage of writing.

Rising action. The progression throughout a story of increasingly dramatic scenes.

Scene. A passage of writing in which the character attempts to achieve a goal.

Scene setup. Information at the beginning of a scene that establishes the character, viewpoint, time, place, and situation, especially as that information relates to the previous passage of writing.

Section. A passage of writing delineated by one or more section breaks.

Section break. A blank line used to signal a change of time, place, or viewpoint.

Segment of writing. Two or more paragraphs with some common purpose. Synonym: passage of writing.

Sensation. The fiction-writing mode for evoking the five senses (sight, hearing, touch, smell, and taste). A *verb of sensation* is a verb used to facilitate a character's sensory perception. For example, *see, hear, feel, smell,* and *taste.*

Sequel. A passage of writing in which the character reflects on the outcome of a scene.

Setting. The "where and when" of a story, including its social, geographic, and political context. Synonym: milieu.

Setup. Writing that informs the reader of the circumstances under which the following passage begins.

Show. Don't tell. A fiction-writing axiom that recommends demonstration over narration.

Simile. A comparison between two things using *like* or *as.* For example, *Number 64, the left tackle, was big and powerful like a tank.*

Sixth sense. Information gained without the aid of sight, hearing, touch, smell, and taste.

Spatial organization. The order in which components of the story's setting are described.

Stakes. Whatever may be gained or lost as a result of a character's effort.

Stimulus. An agent, action, or condition that elicits or accelerates a response.

Style. The "how" of fiction. A composite of the many choices an author makes in the writing of a story.

Structure of a story. The overall conceptual organization of a story. Story structure may be viewed in three parts: macrostructure, midlevel structure, and microstructure. *Macrostructure* is the overarching structure of a story. For example, beginning, middle, and ending. *Midlevel structure* is the arrangement of a story between the macrostructure and the microstructure. For example, scene, transition, and sequel. *Microstructure* is the structure of a story beneath both the macrostructure and the midlevel structure. For example, stimulus, internalization, and response.

Subtext. Meaning beyond the written words and their literal interpretation.

Summarization. The fiction-writing mode of restating actions or events.

Suspended disbelief. A state of the reader's mind in which he perceives himself experiencing or "living" the story.

Suspense. Anxiety caused by uncertainty as to whether, over a period of time, a character will be successful in achieving his goal.

Syntax. The arrangement of words and phrases to create well-formed sentences.

Telling detail. A detail that reveals the essence of that which is being described.

Tension. Anxiety as to whether the character will overcome an obstacle in his attempt to achieve an objective.

Theme. The "why" of a story. A story's underlying meaning or message.

Timeline of a story. A schedule of the events of a story in the order by which they occur. A story's timeline may be divided into three parts: backstory, current story, and future story. *Backstory* includes events relevant to the story but which happen before the written beginning. *Current story* includes events which happen in the "now" of a story, as the tale unfolds. *Future story* includes events that might come after the written ending. For example, characters living happily ever after.

Tone. Word choice reflecting the narrator's attitude toward the subject matter or audience. For example, the tone of writing may be humorous, ominous, scolding, playful, wondrous, instructional, snarky, morbid.

Transition. The fiction-writing mode of moving from one place, time, or character to another.

Verb tense. The verb form that indicates when a written situation takes place. For example, past tense, present tense, and future tense.

Viewpoint character. The person from whose perspective a story segment is told.

Voice. Three types of voice occur in fiction: character voice, narrative voice, and authorial voice. *Character voice* is a character's unique manner of speaking, including inflection, vocabulary, personal speaking habits, and accent, if any. *Narrative voice* is a writing style adopted by the author to tell a particular story. An author may adopt a different style for each story he tells or use the same narrative style for multiple stories. *Author voice* is the author's writing style.

BIBLIOGRAPHY

Bickham, Jack M. *Scene & Structure: How to construct fiction with scene-by-scene flow, logic and readability.* Cincinnati, Ohio: Writer's Digest Books, 1993.

Bickham, Jack M. *The 38 Most Common Fiction Writing Mistakes.* Cincinnati, Ohio: Writer's Digest Books, 1997.

Brown, Dan. *The Da Vinci Code.* New York: Doubleday, 2003.

Card, Orson Scott. *Ender's Game.* Revised mass market edition. New York: Tor, Tom Doherty Associates, LLC, 1994.

Child, Lee. *Without Fail.* Jove premium edition. New York: The Berkley Publishing Group, 2009.

Crichton, Michael. *Jurassic Park.* Paperback. New York: Ballantine Books, 1993.

DeMille, Nelson. *The General's Daughter.* Paperback edition. New York: Warner Books, Inc., 1998.

Evanovich, Janet. *One for the Money*. St. Martin's paperback edition. New York: St. Martin's, 2003.

Flynn, Vince. *American Assassin*. New York: Atria Books, a division of Simon & Schuster, Inc., 2010.

Grisham, John. *The Client*. Paperback. New York: Dell Publishing, 1994.

Ingermanson, Randy and Peter Economy. *Writing Fiction for Dummies*. Hoboken, New Jersey: Wiley Publishing, Inc., 2010.

Meyer, Stephenie. *Twilight*. First media tie-in edition. New York, Little, Brown and Company, 2008.

Obstfeld, Raymond. *Novelist's Essential Guide to Crafting Scenes*. Cincinnati, Ohio: Writer's Digest Books, 2000.

Paulsen, Gary. *Hatchet*. Revised cover edition. New York: Simon & Schuster, 1999.

Random House Dictionary of the English Language, Second Edition, Unabridged. New York: Random House, 1987.

Rosenfeld, Jordan E. *Make a Scene: Crafting a Powerful Story One Scene at a Time*. Cincinnati, Ohio: Writer's Digest Books, 2008.

Sparks, Nicholas. *The Lucky One.* First mass media tie-in edition. New York: Grand Central Publishing, 2012.

Swain, Dwight V. *Techniques of a Selling Writer.* Paperback edition. Norman, Oklahoma: University of Oklahoma Press, 1981.

Webster's Third New International Dictionary of the English Language Unabridged. Springfield, Massachusetts: Merriam-Webster, Inc., 2002.

White, E. B. *Charlotte's Web.* New York: HarperCollins Children's Books, 1980.

INDEX

ENDNOTES

1 *Merriam-Webster Unabridged Dictionary*, scene.

2 Swain, *Techniques of a Selling Writer*, 84.

3 Bickham, *Scene & Structure*, 23.

4 *Merriam-Webster Unabridged Dictionary*, sequel.

5 Swain, *Techniques of a Selling Writer*, 84.

6 Bickham, *Scene & Structure*, 50.

7 Bickham, *Scene & Structure*, 50-51.

8 *Webster's Third New International Dictionary*, motivation.

9 Bickham, *Scene & Structure*, 55.

10 Bickham, *Scene & Structure*, 55.

11 Swain, *Techniques of a Selling Writer*, 97.

12 Swain, *Techniques of a Selling Writer*, 101.

13 Swain, *Techniques of a Selling Writer*, 100.

14 Grisham, *The Client*, 262-265.

15 Card, *Ender's Game*, 1, 9, 16.

16 Bickham, *Scene & Structure*, 55.

17 Swain, *Techniques of a Selling Writer*, 102.

18 Swain, *Techniques of a Selling Writer*, 102.

19 Bickham, *Scene & Structure*, 79.

20 Evanovich, *One for the Money*, 173-174.

21 Grisham, *The Client*, 42-44.

22 Card, *Ender's Game*, 166-168.

23 Bickham, *Scene & Structure*, 79.

24 Bickham, *Scene & Structure*, 79.

25 Bickham, *Scene & Structure*, 79.

26 Sparks, *The Lucky One*, 195-199, 238-241.

27 Sparks, *The Lucky One*, 311-312.

28 Bickham, *Scene & Structure*, 58.

29 Bickham, *Scene & Structure*, 58.

30 Bickham, *Scene & Structure*, 79.

31 Bickham, *Scene & Structure*, 79.

32 Meyer, *Twilight*, 23-27.

33 Meyer, *Twilight*, 269-271.

34 Meyer, *Twilight*, 1.

35 Meyer, *Twilight*, 268-269.

36 Melville, *Moby-Dick*, 27-32.

37 Paulsen, *Hatchet*, 100-103.

38 Grisham, *The Client*, 1-2.

39 Crichton, *Jurassic Park*, 145-147.

40 Melville, *Moby-Dick*, 213-219.

41 White, *Charlotte's Web*, 8-12.

42 Melville, *Moby-Dick*, 161-165.

43 Paulsen, *Hatchet*, 57-61.

44 Brown, *The Da Vinci Code*, 68-70, 91-98, and 157-161.

45 DeMille, *The General's Daughter*, 29-33, 54-65, 78-79.

46 Child, *Without Fail*, 460-473.

47 Bickham, *Scene & Structure*, 72.

48 Brown, *The Da Vinci Code*, 7-11.

49 Card, *Ender's Game*, 1.

50 Flynn, *American Assassin*, 9-12.

51 Grisham, *The Client*.

52 Demille, *The General's Daughter*.

53 Evanovich, *One for the Money*.

54 Sparks, *The Lucky One*, 195-199, 238-241.

55 Crichton, *Jurassic Park*, 79-80.

56 Meyer, *Twilight*, 28.

57 Paulsen, *Hatchet*, 24.

58 Grisham, *The Client*, 88.

59 Meyer, *Twilight*, 195.

60 Card, *Ender's Game*, 96.

61 DeMille, *The General's Daughter*, 40.

62 DeMille, *The General's Daughter*, 98.

63 Sparks, *The Lucky One*, 74.

64 Paulsen, *Hatchet*, 76.

65 Evanovich, *One for the Money*, 88.

66 Paulsen, *Hatchet*, 66.

67 De Mille, *The General's Daughter*, 86.

IF YOU LIKED *SCENES AND SEQUELS*, YOU'LL LOVE *FICTION-WRITING MODES*.

Most books about the craft of writing fiction explain a few fiction-writing modes, but none addresses or even identifies all eleven. *Fiction-Writing Modes: Eleven Essential Tools for Bringing Your Story to Life* is the most comprehensive and concise resource available anywhere regarding fiction-writing modes and the mechanics of presenting them. A *mode* is a particular manner of doing or expressing something. Eleven different modes comprise all written fiction.

Fiction-Writing Modes offers beginning writers an invaluable foundation from which to build skills. This book can help experienced authors reach new levels of success. A better understanding of fiction-writing modes can help any writer understand why some writing works and why some does not.

"One of the most definitive, well-researched approaches to writing fiction that I've ever read. Mike Klaassen has the essential desk reference for fiction writers. Stop what you're writing; read this book, and get ready to apply his eleven modes before you get back to your manuscript. This book will reinvent your writing."

—James V. Smith, Jr., author of the best-selling *You Can Write a Novel*

"If you're looking for the tools that will help you create credible, excellent fiction, look no further. Mike's guide to writing fiction is your light at the end of the tunnel. Stop saying 'I wish I could write a book' and just do it! With Mike's help, you are sure to get there."

—Michael Levin, *New York Times* best-selling author and CEO of BusinessGhost

"Mike Klaassen has created a valuable addition to the working writer's library with his innovative book, *Fiction-Writing Modes*. In it, Klaassen goes beyond most craft books in that he's not only identified eleven writing modes—several of which will be new to readers—but also defines them thoroughly and illustrates how writers can use them to create effective fiction. Highly recommended."

—Les Edgerton, author of *Finding Your Voice*, *Hooked*, and a number of novels and nonfiction works

ORDER YOUR COPY OF *FICTION-WRITING MODES* NOW FROM WHEREVER NEW BOOKS ARE SOLD.

CRACKS

by Mike Klaassen

Five juvenile delinquents on a rampage in the Ozarks of Arkansas. Caves, earthquakes, wild hogs, drugs, knives, guns, and more trouble than anyone should find.

Reading *Cracks* is so intense you want to put it down, but you can't. It is too gripping a read. Mike Klaassen has written another adventurous, powerful book. *Cracks* is a book teen boys will relate to, knowing that there is always hope for their future in spite of the direst circumstances. This book is a must read for young people and for counselors leading youth rehabilitation groups.

—*Midwest Book Review*

When Mike Klaassen couldn't find any books he wanted to read to his sons, he decided to write some. His books are honest and real in the way teenage boys' lives are honest and real. Sometime's there's violence. Sometimes there's gore. But ultimately, the measure of a man is what he carries inside. Mike has a special gift for being able to articulate a boy's inner world without being preachy. If you have a teenage boy you'd like to reach--buy two copies. Give one to your son and read the other. Then sit down and talk. You'll be surprised what happens.

—Cris DiMarco, Author of *Virtual Rock*

ORDER YOUR COPY OF *CRACKS* NOW

FROM WHEREVER NEW BOOKS ARE SOLD.

ABOUT THE AUTHOR

Mike Klaassen is the author of *Backlash: A War of 1812 Novel*, two young-adult novels, and *Fiction-Writing Modes: Eleven Essential Tools for Bringing Your Fiction to Life*. He publishes *For Fiction Writers*, a free monthly ezine about the craft of writing fiction. For more, visit www.mikeklaassen.com